Some Mistakes of Darwin

and a Programmer's Theory of Life

Daniel G. Vintner

Some Mistakes of Darwin and a Programmer's Theory of Life
Copyright © 2022 | Daniel G. Vintner

Cover Art
Szellemek Vitája
Painting by Gyula Boros

Back Cover
Tombs of John Herschel and Charles Darwin
Copyright: Dean and Chapter of Westminster, London

Contributors
Cover design: Gyula Boros Jr.
Illustrator: András Boros Jr.
Developmental editor: Lori DeBoer
Copy editor: Garima Sharma

First edition 2022
Paperback: 978-615-01-2569-5
Kindle: 978-615-01-2571-8
Ebook: 978-615-01-2570-1

danielvintner.com
mail@danielvintner.com

Contents

In Memory of Christopher Eric Hitchens
(13 April 1949–15 December 2011)
Peace Be Upon Him

Introduction

Around 2010, I was browsing a private torrent site on the Web. I can't really remember what I was looking for. I probably wasn't looking for anything particular. Torrent sites offer a variety of freely available and legally questionable products, making them essentially a hub for downloadable content shared by its users. You can find legally distributed products on these sites, but if you were a poor college student like I was, you would have used it to pirate movies and video games. Back then, streaming services and digital distribution were relatively new and not available in most countries; so, if someone wanted to get a product quick and cheap, they would use torrents if they knew how. Not having any cash is also a factor, but while being poor may not excuse my actions, it should explain why I was visiting a torrent site in 2010. As mentioned earlier, I can't really remember what I was looking for at that time. My first illegally downloaded product was Visual Studio, a software created by Microsoft for software engineers. I needed Visual Studio to learn programming, which by that time, I had already been studying for a couple of years. In a way, Visual Studio was my gateway drug to online piracy. By 2010, Visual Studio was freely distributed by Microsoft; so, I was most likely looking for movies and games instead. It usually took hackers a few weeks before they managed to crack a new game, so you never knew in advance when a new game would arrive at the site. However, movies and games were not the only content on this site. There was other stuff as well, such as e-books. I wasn't really interested in books that I had to read on my computer; but, one time, an e-book's title grabbed my attention and I couldn't resist the temptation to read it. Back then, I was clueless about how profoundly this one book would change my views on a certain subject. It was just a book with a weird title. Hence, I downloaded it. I wasn't expecting much from it, just a bit of entertainment. After all, the title of the book was *The Evolution Deceit*.

Until that point, I had never heard anyone ever calling evolution a deceit, or express any kind of doubt in its validity. Not in school, not on TV, and not even by my family and friends. It had simply never happened before, or at least I couldn't recall any such thing ever happening. My parents were and still are atheists, so it should come as no surprise to anyone that I was and still are a non-religious person. My parents, one chemist and one electric engineer, held science in high regard; so, for me the idea of evolution not being anything but well-established scientific truth was both strange and amusing at the same time. Amusing because who in their right mind would deny evolution in 2010? As it turns out, this was something that had been happening quite frequently at that time in other countries, such as the United States; so, it wasn't as much of a novelty as I thought it was, but because I didn't know about the controversy in the United States, I didn't care. So, I started reading. The book was not what I was expecting. Don't get me wrong, it had its weird parts; after all, it was written by a fundamentalist Muslim, but it also presented well-reasoned arguments based on well-researched data. It would be a lie to say that I got convinced then and there, but the arguments were entertaining, and the question eventually did creep into my mind: what if it isn't true? The idea was fascinating and new, or at least for me it was. I had to seriously consider this possibility and acknowledge that the idea had merit. After further introspection, I realized that it not just had merit but also made a lot of sense. You could say that by the time I finished the book, I became a "non-believer." Now, it might not be appropriate to describe me as such, but for me, it certainly felt that way, that my eyes have opened and I have stepped forward into a new world.

I had to share my new discovery with someone, so I gave the e-book to my father, thinking he would surely have the same reaction as I did, or so I believed, but he didn't. And, it wasn't simply the case that he didn't agree with the evidence or conclusions drawn by the author. No, his problems were with the parts of the book that involved philosophical thoughts that were religious in nature, and as far as I can remember, he did not read further than that and never finished the book. These religious parts were the ones that I skimmed through and didn't care much about, but for him, they were a deal-breaker. This was somewhat striking to me as my father was keenly interested in anything related to science, but this was clearly outside of his comfort zone. I would encounter similar reactions a few times more in the future, but I also met a number of people who were more open to entertaining the ideas laid down in the book. Usually, people closer to my age. From this experience, over time, I have come to realize that growing up as an atheist is different from growing into one, and that the first 10 years of your life not only make you but can also break you in some aspects, and this is just as true for me as it is for everyone else.

I regard science and scientists in high esteem; so, you might believe that the denial of a prominent theory would have brought me discomfort, but it didn't. At the time of my conversion, all I could feel was exhilaration. Memories of past ideas also started to resurface from the depths of my mind, along with questions that I had buried deep because I couldn't answer them. For example, in school, I used to think about how easy it is to explain major evolutionary changes by reference to environmental pressure; yet, I could not figure out what the next step of evolution would be for any of the animals we see in nature. Other people didn't seem to be able to do that either, and this struck me as odd. Instead of investigating the question further, I buried my heretical thoughts and forgot about them. I remember other unanswered questions as well, and while the lack of answers could hardly be perceived as reasonable objections to Darwin's theory, it was still surprising to me that they didn't give me pause when I first asked them. Now, these questions would surface in mass and became the pillars of a new worldview that I was comfortable with at the beginning, but much less later on, as after a while, a new feeling, the feeling of doubt took hold of me: What if I made a hasty judgment? After all, I was reading the *Evolution Deceit* and not the *Origin of Species*. The book could be hardly called unbiased. It might have had its facts straight, but I had to wonder, what did it leave out? What other information could be out there that compelled scientists to believe in evolution that I wasn't aware of yet? I had to find out.

So, I started to research the theory, and what I found was more complicated than I hoped it would be. The history of the theory of evolution might seem to be a straight road to the casual observer, but it really isn't. It is more like a jungle path filled with obstacles that change every time you take it. Despite all the obstacles, I believe I managed to get a good grasp of the modern theory of evolution and of its history. The same time I was researching evolution, I also tried to find people who, like me, were in doubt. I learned that in the United States, there was a controversial movement called the Intelligent Design (ID) movement, which became notorious for its involvement in a court case regarding educational material selected for a state school in Dover, Pennsylvania. This happened in 2005, and even the then president George W. Bush gave his verbal support to the idea of teaching alternative theories alongside evolution. Needless to say, this has not come to pass, and I have only learned about the plaintiff's victory who argued against the alternative theory long after the trial was over. The ideas ID brought to the table were interesting, but not without their own flaws, and while the fundamental idea is worthy of serious consideration and objective research, the movement and its teachings carry with it intellectual baggage that is hard to not notice and, consequently, tolerate.

Over time, I have developed my own critique of Darwin's theory based on my own reasoning and views. I realized that my way of looking at things was in some ways unique, as not many seemed to share the views I had. Even the few who shared my views had different reasons for having them and looked at the facts from a different perspective than I did. I don't like writing very much, unless its software, of course; so, if there was another book out there like this, I would have been content sharing that with other people, but there wasn't. Hence, I decided to write my own book, despite the fact that I'm in no way an expert in biology. I believed that someone might find my opinion and reasoning on this subject interesting enough to actually buy and appreciate a book of this kind. So, that's what I did: I wrote a book cover to cover. Then, I threw out the whole thing because it took so long to write it that by the end of it, I wasn't satisfied with my work. In my opinion, it was good, just not good enough for me to actually get it published. I decided to rewrite it, but shuffling between my programming job and writing was a losing battle for me; so, my second attempt at writing was delayed considerably. If I learned one thing from Darwin it was that you need to be patient when you attempt to write a book of this kind. Many people write their books while having a full-time job, but for me this approach never worked. People view me as an eccentric person, and they are right to see me as such; the way I would put it is that I have a one-track mind, it may be a very wide track, but at the end of the day, it is still just one track. That's the best I can describe it. It may be a programmer's disease that I have trouble focusing on more than one thing, but only God knows if that is, indeed, the case and I am not just imagining it to be so. Eventually, my day job resulted in financial stability that allowed me to quit my job once more and focus my efforts on writing again. That is until I felt that that stability was gone and started working again; but, if you are reading these lines somewhere on paper or your laptop after visiting a torrent site, then you can assume that this second attempt was more successful than the first.

Unfortunately, any attempt at a review of the theory of evolution seems to generate more debate than research or results of any kind. It is a curious phenomenon related to the fact that Darwin's magnum opus and similar works attempt to explain not just the origin of species but of humans as well, and this makes it not just interesting, but personal for many people for various reasons. The phenomenon is curious because when a new theory or a new version of an old theory is proposed, the initial reaction often seems to be "why is this person proposing this?" rather than "what is the evidence for it?" If someone proposes a new string theory, you can be sure that the former question will not be asked, regardless of how bad this person's theory is and how faulty his methods are. The politicization of science is not unique to evolution. It happens anyplace where the fate of humankind is involved in some manner; however, in truth few theories have less consequences for the prosperity of man than the theory of evolution. How we got here won't change where we are or the fact that we are here. If you or the majority of the population holds some genuinely bad ideas regarding this topic, it will not harm the people who hold those views or society, but as there is no harm, there is also no simple way to recognize the existence of those bad ideas. This can make it challenging to root out bad ideas and, in my opinion, this perhaps more than anything is the source of the underlying problem. There's about a one in a billion chance that you will agree with all or most of the arguments laid out in this book; so, the chance that you will disagree with some of it is very high. The point I wish to make is that for anyone to enjoy this book, it pretty much requires to have an active mind rather than a closed or even open mind. It is much more crucial to think about the ideas rather than to agree with them—to see facts for what they are and to consider the value of arguments based on their merit. It does not matter whether I argue for or against an idea, and it should not matter whether you agree with it or not. Critical thinking should be applied in all cases.

Many people believe that we have found a good and

possibly final theory in evolution. That it sorts of fulfills the scientific requirements and fits the natural world and our expectations, and that we don't really need alternative theories or even criticism of the theory. The idea is that we are past the evaluation phase of the theory, that it has won and, therefore, it should be accepted as fact or at least as close to factual as scientific thought allows. If you believe that I am exaggerating, then I would like to highlight that one notable biologist claimed that evolution is the same kind of "fact" as the fact that "the Earth revolves around the Sun" and the same person compared the hubris of evolution skeptics to that of Holocaust deniers. The skeptics, in this case, were the proponents of Intelligent Design mentioned earlier, but we can assume that all deniers and doubters fall into the same category as long as they don't agree with the major tenets of evolution. Such an approach to criticism may not always be proper, even if the new theory is badly structured or lacking in some other aspects that prevent the application of scientific inquiry. Even bad ideas should be heard and considered and not for the sake of openness but for the sake of objectivity.

This book will start where everything started, with Darwin, and it will examine what his original theory was really about and why he came to the conclusions that he did. We discover where the origin of the *Origin* truly was and whether Darwin lived up to the principles he borrowed from his peers. After Darwin, we will follow the theory of evolution over the centuries and discover how much it has really transformed and how much of Darwin's original theory has remained intact to our present time. In addition, we will discover how some of the problems of evolution that have not been solved by Darwin were not solved by the people who came after him and have been mostly forgotten by contemporary researchers. To get to the bottom of why these problems have persisted for centuries, we must discover how life works and what are the fundamental building blocks of organisms so that we can truly understand what evolution can and cannot be responsible for in nature. We will look at every piece of evidence the theory of evolution has to offer and ascertain if they would still hold up if they were presented to an unbiased audience who were not indoctrinated by the popular beliefs of the past. To test evolution, we will discuss what tests, if any, can be done to verify the theory and what it would mean to any theory in science if such tests could not be done to verify them. And, last but not least, we will compare evolution to any alternative theory we can find to determine what merits it has over the other and discover whether the theory of evolution is any different from the pseudoscientific ideas of the past two millennia. Given the subject of this book, I can almost guarantee that sooner or later, it will hurt the feelings of any reader, but I can promise that the radical ideas presented by this book are not meant to deceive you but to engage you to think about the things we believe to know in a different light.

I believe the best defense of heretical ideas came from the late British journalist Christopher Hitchens in a debate titled, "Freedom of Speech includes the Freedom to Hate" where Hitchens brilliantly defended free speech as an absolute right. His defense is available online, and I believe every human being should watch it at least once in their lifetime. It is not difficult to find. Simply search "Christopher Hitchens free speech" on the Internet. Hitchens notes the work of past liberal philosophers and builds his argument based on theirs:

> "It is not just the right of the person who speaks to be heard, it is the right of everyone in the audience to listen and to hear and every time you silence somebody you make

yourself a prisoner of your own actions, because you deny your right to hear something."

Then, he describes a textbook Holocaust denier and adds:

"...that person doesn't just have a right to speak, that person's right to speak must be given extra protection, because what he has to say must have taken him some effort to come up with. Might contain a grain of historical truth. Might in any case give people to think about why they know what they already think they know. How do I know this except that I've always been told this and never heard anything else. It's always worth establishing first principles. It's always worth saying what would you do if you met a Flat Earth Society member. Come to think of it how can I prove that the Earth is round? Am I sure about the theory of evolution? I know it's supposed to be true. Here's someone who says there's no such thing, it's all intelligent design. How sure am I of my own views?"

Christopher Hitchens was defending the right to free speech, but it is clear from his defense that the true beneficiary of speech is not the speaker but the listener. Moreover, the listener can not only be prevented from listening by the actions of others but also by the actions or inaction of the listener himself. The listener can always choose to not listen or not think about new ideas. He can always choose to disregard everything that is being heard by him regardless of the merit it may have. This is why Hitchens warns his audience:

"... Don't take refuge in the false security of consensus and the feeling that whatever you think you're bound to be okay because you're in the safe moral majority."

This is the warning I also intend to give to you before you read this book or any other controversial material for that matter. If we disregard any idea before it is presented to us, then we will never find any *"grain of historical truth,"* much less realize the real truth, wherever or whenever it might present itself to us.

Chapter 1

The Age of Darwin

I magine living in the Victorian era of the nineteenth century in Britain. The setting is modern from a historical viewpoint but is, simultaneously, very much steeped in tradition. The scientific and industrial revolutions have transformed medieval Britain into a modern state with great power; however, after the Age of Enlightenment, religion and spiritualism made a comeback. The Catholic Church, especially, had its next renaissance at this time in Britain. So, this is where you live, in an educated yet somewhat superstitious society at the end of the Enlightenment. Now imagine being a respected naturalist who came from a wealthy family and, through hard work, has gained the respect of other naturalists and an enviable status in the community. This is your situation, but you are about to smash one of the last foundations of the Christian faith that have remained strong throughout the Enlightenment, and you have to work out how to do this without destroying your own credibility and your family's good name. Obviously, you cannot start this fight unprepared. The stakes are high, and you cannot expect much leniency from the believers and even less from the naturalists, and the fact that the ideologies of these two groups overlap will not make your job any easier.

This was the dilemma Charles Darwin faced. His theory of evolution could have been interpreted as going against the dominant view of the era, which was creationism. At this time, it was widely believed that living beings were created by God and arguments for the existence of God, such as the teleological argument, supported this interpretation of creation and creator. The watchmaker analogy, which was introduced by William Paley in the early 1800s, was a popular defense for the argument from design. Essentially, this hypothesis suggested that if a watch was found on a sandy beach, no one would expect it to be the work of natural forces but of a watchmaker. Furthermore, given that living beings are at least as intricate as modern watches, our expectations for the origin of either should be very similar. This argument did not employ any religious authority but implied that a creator God, indeed, existed, thereby making it the most favorable explanation for the naturalists, who then were still predominantly religious.

Darwin was not the first to introduce the idea that species descended from each other, and that natural selection was the driving force behind this process. Others might have come before, but Darwin was the first who presented the idea in a concise manner, supported by observable evidence. For example, the book *Vestiges* (*Vestiges of the Natural History of Creation*) became a best seller but was widely criticized and dismissed as unscientific, and the author remained anonymous for decades after its release. Evolution by natural selection was a strong idea, but Darwin had to describe it in a palatable way to naturalists and theologians alike.

One of the most ingenious and somewhat questionable methods he used was an attempt to shift the burden of questioning God onto a well-known and well-respected natural philosopher who also happened to be a devout Christian. This way, Darwin could always point to someone else if theological issues were raised regarding his theory because a naysayer would have had to criticize not just Darwin but also one of the greatest minds of the era. Whether this worked practically remains debatable, but Darwin did certainly try. He starts the introduction to his *Origin of Species* with these words: "WHEN ONBOARD H.M.S. 'BEAGLE,' as naturalist, I was much struck with certain facts in the distribution of the inhabitants of South America, and in the geological relations of the present to the past inhabitants of that continent. These facts seemed to me to throw some light on the origin of species —that mystery of mysteries, as it has been called by one of our greatest philosophers." The philosopher mentioned by Darwin was John Herschel and he was quite right to call the origin of species "that mystery of mysteries" and Herschel "one of our greatest philosophers."

Before we delve deeper into this mystery, let us discuss in further detail the relationship between Darwin and Herschel, as it will reveal a surprising level of insights into Darwin's greatest accomplishment. Darwin was first introduced to Herschel while attending college at Cambridge, where he read Herschel's *Preliminary Discourse on the Study of Natural Philosophy*. This book was the principal work on the philosophy of science until a book called *System of Logic*, written by John Stuart Mill, overshadowed it. Mill acknowledged that the central chapters of his book were based on Herschel's earlier book. Both Mill and Herschel were empiricists who favored experimentation as a means to validate scientific theories, and Herschel, in particular, had a substantial impact on Darwin's beliefs. Darwin would later write in his autobiography that the *Discourse* was one of two books that "stirred up in me a burning zeal to add even the most humble contribution to the noble structure of natural science." The quote from Herschel that Darwin chooses to put into the first paragraph of his book is quite revealing in this regard. The words originated from a letter Herschel sent, not to Darwin, but Darwin's friend, the geologist Charles Lyell. In this letter, Herschel praises Lyell for his *Principles of Geology*, which according to the letter, Herschel had read three times. In this book, Lyell alludes to the idea that species might have originated from one another, but he did not commit to the idea, fearing the potential blowback. However, Herschel was less concerned about possible criticism and wrote to Lyell:

> He that on such quest would go must know nor fear nor failing. To coward soul or faithless heart the search were unavailing — Of course I allude to that **mystery of mysteries** the replacement of extinct species by others. Many will doubtless think your speculations too bold — but it is as well to face the difficulty at once. For my own part — I cannot but think it an inadequate conception of the Creator, to assume it as granted that his combinations are exhausted upon any one of the theatres of their former exercise — though in this, as in all his other works we are led by all analogy to suppose that he operates through a series of intermediate causes & that in consequence, the origination of fresh species, could it ever come under our cognizance would be found to be a natural in contradistinction to a miraculous process — although we perceive no indication of any process actually in progress which is likely to issue in such a result.

This paragraph of Herschel's letter was quite revolutionary for its time and must have undoubtedly raised quite a few eyebrows when it was first published in 1837 in the Appendices to *Babbage's Ninth Bridgewater Treatise* about a year after Darwin's voyage on the Beagle had ended. Darwin could use Herschel's words as a shield, deflecting unwanted and unwarranted criticism owing to Herschel's overwhelming stature and credibility as a philosopher of science. Even Lyell acknowledged to William Whewell that if he had said what Herschel wrote in the letter then, he would "have raised a host of prejudices" against himself, but by publishing Hershel's letter, both Lyell and Darwin could easily sidestep the opposition to "these mysterious subjects."

Herschel's insight was crucial for two reasons. One, he acknowledged that a species might turn into another via a process guided by natural law, and two, God could use this law as a means for creating a new species, thereby keeping this proposed new law in the realm of natural theology and preventing any accusation of spreading heretical ideas. Of course, Darwin did not say that God was necessary for evolution to exist nor did he want to say it or even believe such a thing, but he most likely understood the importance of this justification, for the people who were already familiar with the letter or could be enlightened, if necessary. Here, I would also like to highlight that the phrase "*the origination of fresh species*" that Herschel wrote in his letter sounds remarkably similar to the title Darwin chose to give his book, perhaps, because this is where it, in fact, came from. We know that Herschel found Lyell's work remarkable, calling it a "revolution in their subject," which was high praise coming from him, but Herschel was not the only one influenced by Lyell's book. At the beginning of his voyage on the Beagle, Darwin also read Lyell's *Principles of Geology*, which was no doubt instrumental to the development of Darwin's own theory of natural selection.

Lyell championed two key concepts in his foundational work on geology—uniformitarianism and gradualism. Uniformitarianism simply states that the processes that formed the Earth's surface over time are the same ones we can observe today. The subtitle of *Principles of Geology* reflects this idea clearly: "being an attempt to explain the former changes of the Earth's surface, by reference to causes now in operation." During the time Lyell wrote his book, most geologists favored the theory of catastrophism, which was the idea that most geological features appeared abruptly and violently. According to this theory, the Earth did not have to be more than a few thousand years old. Although catastrophism was an idea that did not question the theological concept that the Earth was less than 6000 years old, what Lyell suggested did. He proposed the idea of gradualism, as most observable changes in geology were slow and gradual, and consistent with the principle of uniformitarianism, those gradual changes had to be responsible for the alterations of the Earth's surface. Catastrophists, for example, believed that a volcano gained height because of new mass forming on the top of the volcano during an eruption, while gradualists believed that the pressure building up under the surface of the volcano was the real reason why volcanoes would rise from the Earth's crust. While Lyell wasn't correct about everything, his work became one of the foundations of modern geology, which recognized that most changes happen slowly over time, even though some happen abruptly and with great destructive power. The issue with catastrophism was that it was too speculative, which made geology less exact and, consequently, less scientific. Conversely, the issue with gradualism was that it was too exclusive and tried to explain the results of catastrophic events by reference to gradual change, even when that could not be done. That said, the limitation of gradualism was much less severe "or catastrophic" as pure speculation and, therefore, easier to fix.

Lyell's theory of gradualism was a science built on empirical observations, and this is what Herschel saw when he read *Principles of Geology*. As Herschel was one of the great empiricists of the time, it is easy to understand why he was pleased with the book. Despite his fondness for Lyell's work, when the geologists of the two opposing sides clashed, Herschel refused to take a stand and didn't involve himself in the debate. Perhaps, he recognized that while Lyell's theories were fundamentally correct in their approach, the actual results were not necessarily supported by adequate observable evidence. Herschel, who was a true classical polymath, well versed in and a contributor to many scientific fields, was keenly aware of how hard it was to establish a scientific theory and how hard it was to determine its correctness. His experience and understanding of the philosophy of science most likely granted him the wisdom that most scientists to this day often lack. He was a realist to the bitter end, and even beyond. In the Discourse, Herschel wrote the following regarding the science of geology:

> But to estimate justly the effects of causes now in action in geology is no easy task. There is no à priori or deductive process by which we can estimate the amount of the annual erosion, ... nor the quantity of lava thrown up per annum by volcanoes over the whole surface of the earth, nor any similar effect. And to consult experience on all such points is a slow and painful process if rightly gone into, and a very fallible one if only partially executed. Much, then, at present must be left to opinion, and to that

sort of clear-judging tact which sometimes anticipates experience; but this ought not to stand in the way of our making every possible effort to obtain accurate information on such points, by which alone geology can be rendered, if not an experimental science, at least a science of that kind of active observation which forms the nearest approach to it, where actual experiment is impossible.

Lyell was slightly less reserved in his approach to geology and had by then challenged the orthodox view of a young Earth. While this didn't bother Herschel, it most certainly bothered others. The Christian view of a 6000-old Earth was not necessarily well-grounded, even by theological standards. The age of the Earth was not written down in Genesis clearly and concisely, so challenging the figure of 6000 was relatively mild, compared with what Darwin was about to unleash with his own ideas.

Before Darwin came along, the popular theory for the origin of species involved a quick and abrupt creation, which was not too different from the idea of catastrophism in geology. Darwin's idea of evolution by natural selection used the same uniformitarian perspective Lyell championed, but instead of applying it to geology, Darwin applied the idea of gradual change of living organisms to biology. This was something that Lyell had also considered and alluded to in his book, but it was Darwin who did all the research and followed the idea to its logical conclusions, including being willing to publish his controversial views with his name on the cover. No doubt Darwin was inspired by Herschel's words: "He that on such quest would go must know nor fear nor failing. To coward soul or faithless heart the search were unavailing." He certainly forged himself an iron will so that he could push his idea through all the obstacles and opposition. His goal was to challenge and overrule an idea that had stood the test of time for more than a millennium. To say that Darwin had to fight an uphill battle would be an understatement. Even while working on his book, he was often sick, quite possibly because of stress. Nevertheless, he stayed on course, believing that by applying Lyell's gradualism to biological organisms, he could present a strong argument for natural selection and win this great debate for the future of science.

If we track the progression of evolutionary thought from its inception to the present, we realize that both its greatest strength and greatest weakness have come from the *Origin of Species*. Darwin's book was constructed in a very deliberate, straightforward, and—most of all—logical manner. Each chapter in the first half of the book ends exactly where the next one needs to begin, as if each chapter was an introduction for the one coming after it. The theory is short and simple, but the explanation is long and arduous. We must not forget that the *Origin of Species* was written for an audience that had most likely never heard about the theory of evolution before. Moreover, we who possess the power of hindsight must be careful not to color Darwin's words with our modern views on the subject. If we want to understand what message Darwin really wanted to convey and what his theories were about, then it would be a good idea to imagine what an informed British subject living in the Victorian era would have thought about Darwin's writing.

In the first chapter, "Variation Under Domestication," Darwin discusses the history of domesticated plants and animals. Darwin explains how different species were changed by breeders over time. They would select individual specimens from a group and only let the ones with desirable characteristics breed with each other and have offspring, thereby increasing the dominance of those characteristics inside the group. By comparing domesticated plants and animals to their natural counterparts, Darwin accentuates that domestication leads to much greater variation and could greatly change the attributes and behavior of the domesticated breeds compared with the original specimens. From the examples Darwin gives, we can extrapolate that (i) species can and do change their characteristics over time, and (ii) selection is the indirect cause of change.

Darwin used the term "artificial selection" for the process of breeding later in the book, but generally the idea of selection is artificial by nature and, thus, does not require the "artificial" attribute, except when it must be distinguished from the concept of natural selection. Hence, Darwin used the artificial label in the fourth chapter, "Natural Selection," but we should not pretend that selection is a standard natural process by default. Generally, the action of selection always requires a conscious agent that can decide the condition for selection, or at the very least can select objects from a group that meet a specific criterion. Breeders select specimens with more advantageous characteristics for achieving the breeder's goal. An animal breeder, for example, selects animals that produce more milk, meat, or wool. In addition, breeders can select animals that are faster or stronger than their competition if being faster or stronger is desired. In Darwin's book, the process of breeding serves as an analogy for natural selection, but he needed to establish a few more facts before he could present his main argument. This being the case, we must not forget why the first chapter discusses the concept of selection, and that selective breeding is not an example of evolution by natural selection but a process that is very similar to it, but not quite the same. We might see it as an example, but someone who has never heard about evolution certainly would not.

The second chapter, "Variation Under Nature," moves

quickly from domesticated animals and plants to wild plants and animals. Darwin primarily focuses on the confusion regarding the distinction between a variety and a species, which was a relevant topic in naturalist circles during his time. He discusses the question of when does a variety become classified as new species and under what circumstances should it stay in the same subgroup instead, or vice versa. To this day, it is difficult to specify what exactly constitutes a species, so we can imagine how challenging the situation was for the biologists during Darwin's time. Darwin highlights that species with many varieties also tend to be related to many more species compared with those that have few varieties. Notably, the only thing differentiating a variation from species for Darwin is a "Divergence of Character," rather than the ability to produce fertile offspring. Given this confusion in the classification and how our understanding has evolved in this area, we should be a little more wary about drawing any conclusions regarding this matter. Whether the claim that more varieties equate more species was proven in Darwin's time remains debatable, but either way, his main point stands: varieties are a possible precursor to the appearance of new species. In addition, there can be no doubt that domesticated species change in the same way they change in nature. Let me reiterate: species do change, and new variations do emerge via change all the time. Darwin argued in later chapters that this change has, over a very long period of time, created all species in existence and, therefore, this is how species must originate in nature.

In the third chapter, Darwin introduces the idea of the "Struggle for Existence," and he concludes that this struggle is why natural selection must exist. Every group of a particular species tends to grow in number, but they cannot multiply indefinitely because there's a limit to the food available in their environment; this causes specimens to compete with other organisms inside and even outside of their group, resulting in a struggle for existence for each group and for each member of a group. A group, in this case, can comprise several distinct species, as in nature many different species rely on each other to survive and cannot survive without each other. By introducing the idea of the struggle for existence and the concepts preceding it, Darwin has laid down all the groundwork he needed to present his main argument.

These three chapters build to the fourth chapter, which is titled with the name of Darwin's new idea: "Natural Selection." In it, Darwin asks the following questions: "HOW will the struggle for existence, discussed too briefly in the last chapter, act in regard to variation? Can the principle of selection, which we have seen is so potent in the hands of man, apply in nature?" The answer, in Darwin's opinion, is natural selection. He claims that natural selection produces the same results as artificial selection, except that it is not guided by an intelligent agent, and, unlike artificial selection, it does not only take into account the needs of the species but also the needs of other interrelated species in the ecosystem as well. Nature selects the varieties that are more likely than others to survive; this concept will later be called the "survival of the fittest." Darwin believed that, over time, these varieties would become so distinct from their ancestors that they would no longer be able to breed with each other and will, therefore, become new species, and that is what evolution by natural selection is truly about. Darwin summarizes this idea as such:

> If during the long course of ages and under varying conditions of life, organic beings vary at all in the several parts of their organization, and I think this cannot be disputed; if there be, owing to the high geometrical powers of increase

of each species, at some age, season, or year, a severe struggle for life, and this certainly cannot be disputed; then, considering the infinite complexity of the relations of all organic beings to each other and to their conditions of existence, causing an infinite diversity in structure, constitution, and habits, to be advantageous to them, I think it would be a most extraordinary fact if no variation ever had occurred useful to each being's own welfare, in the same way as so many variations have occurred useful to man. But if variations useful to any organic being do occur, assuredly individuals thus characterized will have the best chance of being preserved in the struggle for life; and from the strong principle of inheritance they will tend to produce offspring similarly characterized. This principle of preservation, I have called, for the sake of brevity, Natural Selection.

Darwin concludes his main argument for natural selection, delineating what type of natural phenomena causes variation and how in the following chapter, "Laws of Variation." This, of course, is a critical question, as we want to know what type of natural phenomena causes variation and how. The theory of evolution does not require this knowledge *per se*, but it is certainly in the interest of science to gain this information, as it helps us better understand the greater process. In the twentieth century, the rediscovery of Mendel's laws of inheritance solved this issue for the most part, but prior to the advent of genetics, as long as one could observe the appearance of new forms in nature, it was acceptable to not dig any deeper than that. This is pretty much what Darwin thought:

Whatever the cause may be of each slight difference in the offspring from their parents – and a cause for each must exist – it is the steady accumulation, through natural selection, of such differences, when beneficial to the individual, that gives rise to all the more important modifications of structure, by which the innumerable beings on the face of this earth are enabled to struggle with each other, and the best adapted to survive.

If we think back to Lyell's uniformitarian idea of the present being the key to the past, as well as his gradualist approach to natural phenomena, we can clearly see that Darwin's argument closely follows his methodology and principles. The first six chapters are the salient of the book, as they contain Darwin's proof for his theory of natural selection. This proof is Darwin's main scientific argument, and the chapter following the sixth already deals with "Difficulties on Theory," which is, strictly speaking, not part of the main argument. Only after dealing with the objections he anticipates will be raised by his opposition does he continue to offer further facts and arguments in line with his theory. Most of these are what one could call the arguments for the tree of life, which contains the argument from geological distribution, the argument from fossils, and the argument from morphology. Assuming that the hierarchy of the tree of life is correct, and it undoubtedly is to a very high degree, any origin of species theory must corroborate that fact. Darwin's theory certainly fulfills this requirement, but being consistent with the tree of life is not necessarily sufficient to prove that it is correct. This, undoubtedly, makes the theory more plausible, especially compared with other less-sophisticated theories, but the uniformitarian doctrine requires observable phenomena in the present and not in the distant past. Else, there won't be anything that could be independently verified. To clarify this point further, let us read a part of Darwin's letter to George Bentham, dated May 22, 1863:

In fact the belief in natural selection must at present be grounded entirely on general considerations. (1) on its being a *vera causa*, from the struggle for existence; & the certain geological fact that species do somehow change (2) from the analogy of change under domestication by man's selection. (3) & chiefly from this view connecting under an intelligible point of view a host of facts.

Darwin's argument seems to rest almost exclusively on the first five chapters: "Variation Under Domestication," "Variation Under Nature," "Struggle for Existence," "Natural Selection," and "Laws of Variation." The letter Darwin wrote confirms this, as it does not reference the later chapters in any way that is not indirect. This letter is also crucial because it proves that Darwin did, in fact, read Herschel's *Preliminary Discourse* and that he was influenced by him, as the concept of *"vera causa"* that his letter to Bentham mentions comes directly from that book. *Vera causa* can be translated as "a true cause," which refers to the ultimate cause of a specific natural phenomenon.

Darwin was a big admirer of Herschel and his work. He cared much about his opinion, so he was naturally interested in what Herschel thought about the *Origin of Species*. No doubt he was hoping that Herschel would acknowledge him and endorse the book, just as he had done with Lyell and his book. Unfortunately for Darwin, Herschel was not as amazed by the *Origin* as he was by *Principles of Geology* two decades earlier. Perhaps, this is an understatement, as after Darwin published his book, Herschel called natural selection the "law of higgledy-piggledy," which dissatisfied Darwin greatly. Darwin even sent a copy to Herschel with a personal note praising Herschel's work, hoping that he would read his new book. Well, Herschel did read it, and his reaction was clearly not what Darwin was hoping for. When Darwin learned what Herschel called his theory, he wrote to Lyell that this was a "great blow and discouragement." We can imagine how big of a disappointment this must have been for him. Darwin was like the messiah that Herschel had called for, but when Darwin had arrived and finished what was expected of him, he was disavowed by the one who summoned him.

What could have been Herschel's reason for rejecting Darwin's idea? Was it because Darwin did not invoke God as an agent to create life or for the law that was supposed to create life? Herschel was okay with a law made by God to create new species, so shouldn't he regard natural selection favorably in some form or another? We might look down on Herschel for suggesting the idea that any law required a god's involvement, but we must not forget that the post-Enlightenment era had a unique view regarding God and God's relationship to nature. Today, most academics do not believe in the existence of any type of god, but the majority of scientists at the time were believers. Even the second-most popular stance was not disbelief, but deism, which was a belief in God that rejected the authenticity of revelation. In this world of religious scientists, the dominant worldview most naturalists held was natural theology. God was the creator of not just the universe but its laws as well. For example, the law of gravity was believed to be ordained by God. Such divine laws not only guided human action but also compelled nature to act in a certain way. It was a law of God, not a moral law, that guided human action, but a law nonetheless and one that compelled nature to act in a certain way. These were not just nature's laws, but God's as well, for all natural theologians. That was the norm. For example, the *Ninth Bridgewater Treatise*, a work of natural theology, was a continuation of a series commissioned by the Earl of Bridgewater to explore "the

Power, Wisdom, and Goodness of God, as manifested in the Creation." Coincidentally, it contains the letter penned by Herschel that Darwin would later quote in the *Origin*.

A few months before Darwin's *Origin of Species* arrived in the bookstores, Herschel's own book, *Physical Geography,* was published. In this book, Herschel expressed that new, more complex species would eventually replace old ones over time, but that this process was neither gradual nor abrupt. Rather, he believed that new and old species would live together for a while before eventually some would die out and disappear from the Earth. This completely differed from what Darwin suggested in the *Origin*, and in 1861, Herschel added a lengthy footnote to the revised edition of his book about his own opinion regarding Darwin's theory of evolution. Once the second edition was complete, he sent a signed copy to Darwin. The footnote he added is a bit complicated, so I will try to provide an explanation as we go through the text. However, be warned that this will be only my interpretation of Herschel's words and might differ from his true intent and opinion.

> This was written previous to the publication of Mr. Darwin's work on the *Origin of Species*, a work which, whatever its merit or ingenuity, we cannot, however, consider as having disproved the view taken in the text. We can no more accept the principle of arbitrary and casual variation of natural selection as a sufficient condition, per se, of the past and present organic world, than we can receive the Laputan method of composing books (pushed l'outrance) as a sufficient account of Shakespeare and the Principia...

These words are quite harsh, considering that what

Herschel calls the Laputan method is something the fictional "projectors in speculative learning" used to generate new works of art and science in the novel *Gulliver's Travels*. As harsh as it may seem, Herschel used an insightful analogy that shines a light on the arbitrary nature of Darwin's idea. In the novel, one professor of speculative learning creates a machine that contains all words in all possible forms and, when the machine is turned on, it assigns the words into several lines. Once this was done, someone would read the lines and, if some of the words in a line made a sentence fragment, that fragment would be written down by several scribes. This process would repeat itself, and the results would be collected into large volumes. The creator of the machine intended to copy the fragments into new works of science and art to create every book of the past, present, and future. It is hard to imagine that anything worthy of reading would be created using such a haphazard method that yielded mostly unintelligible results. The message Herschel wanted to convey with this analogy is that there's no fundamentally good reason to believe that arbitrary variation would produce new forms in nature or anywhere else, for that matter. The Laputan method is certainly not a perfect analogy, but Jonathan Swift could not have predicted, a century before Darwin, that his fictional characters would take part in a scientific debate. The method falls short because while only good fragments are collected by the scribes, they are not organized by a simple guiding principle such as natural selection; however, this problem can be fixed using a different method to assemble the desired new works of art and science. Instead of collecting the generated fragments in large volumes, we can incrementally add them to a manuscript based on what fragment from the generated ones would fit the fragments already located in a specific manuscript. We would start with an empty manuscript and repeat the process until we obtain a complete book. This way, we could assemble a new book simply by generating new fragments and always adding the "fittest" to our growing manuscript. The question is: would such a process produce anything that is of equal value to the works of Shakespeare and Newton, and if not, why should we treat the idea of natural selection creating a new species differently? Herschel continues:

> Equally in either case, an intelligence, guided by a purpose, must be continually in action to bias the directions of the steps of change – to regulate their amount – to limit their divergence – and continue them in a definite course. We do not believe that Mr. Darwin means to deny the necessity of such intelligent direction. But it does not, so far as we can see, enter into the formula of his law; and without it we are unable to conceive how the law can have led to the results. On the other hand, we do not mean to deny that such intelligence may act according to law (that is to say, on a preconceived and definite plan). Such law, stated in words, would be no other than the actual observed law of organic succession; or one more general, taking that form when applied to our own planet, and including all the links of the chain which have disappeared. But the one laws is a necessary supplement to the other, and ought, in all logical propriety, to form a part of its enunciation. Granting this, and with some demur as to the genesis of man, we are far from disposed to repudiate the view taken of this mysterious subject in Mr. Darwin's work.

In other words, if God does not guide the creation of new species directly, there must be a law of succession that is either observable in the present or in the past through the examination of organisms living today or the fossil record. Besides, if the latter can be done, then the former is also possible to some extent, as they are interdependent. This law of succession must be different from Darwin's law of variation, or even Mendel's law of inheritance, as it must describe how one species becomes another rather than how species vary, or which characteristics are more or less likely to be inherited. These conditions for the law of succession may seem difficult or even impossible, but without such requirements, the theory cannot be verified and, thus, we cannot determine to what extent natural selection is responsible for the origination of new species. Darwin might have found a *vera causa* in natural selection; however, in Herschel's opinion, limiting our interest to a single specific true cause is only the beginning of the inductive process. The cause must be verified, and that usually encompasses the necessity of predicting the direction and extent of the cause producing the phenomena and then comparing that to nature itself. Even for events happening thousands or even millions of years in the past, this fundamental scientific principle must be followed to establish the adequacy of the *vera causa* and the validity of the hypothesis.

If you still doubt that Herschel's critique is correct, consider the following thought experiment. Would you believe that someone could throw a water bottle as far as the International Space Station (ISS) is from Earth, just because the person said they could? This person can, in fact, throw a bottle as far as 10, 11, and even 12 meters, which means that they can throw $n+1$ meters and could potentially throw as far as 408,000 meters, which is how far the ISS is. This individual might claim that the fact that there are any water bottles on the ISS is proof that they can throw that far, and they do not need to demonstrate the process in action. We could counter this argument by stating that they need to establish the "extent" of their power, as it might diminish as the distance increases, and to do so in the correct "direction," because throwing a bottle from Earth to the ISS is not the same as throwing the same bottle from the ISS to Earth. Therefore, we would require proof of the extent and of direction, just as Herschel would have wanted, and the claimant would need to figure out how they would do that, not us.

Darwin wrote one last letter to Herschel. Although just as polite and graceful as Darwin's other letters, this letter was most certainly not the best he had ever written, for he tried to dodge the issue and refused to meet Herschel's argument head-on. In the first part of the letter, he mentioned the work he and the American botanist Asa Gray had done in relation to the issue of "intelligent design," and he also suggested strongly that he did not see any evidence or the need to involve God's interference to explain his theory. This is a counterpoint to the first part of Herschel's critique, but Darwin never dealt with or even acknowledged the second objection Herschel raised against the theory of evolution, which was related to the direction and extent natural selection could drive evolution. Instead, in the second part of his letter, Darwin expressed his confidence that his theory would win in the long run and that this confidence came from the fact that many naturalists had already expressed support for his theory. Even if we ignore this second part, the question remains: why didn't Darwin respond to all of the objections Herschel raised? He certainly had no issue with disagreeing with Herschel and putting those objections into words, so why did he ignore the second part of Herschel's critique, which was, by all accounts, more important than the first? Perhaps, an earlier letter Darwin sent, not to Herschel, but to the aforementioned Asa Gray, can provide us with more insights into Darwin's true beliefs on this matter. The letter discusses natural selection and was sent on November 29, 1857, two years before the publication of the *Origin of Species*:

> This shall be such an extraordinary note as you have never received from me, for it shall not contain one single question or request. I thank you for your impression on my views. Every criticism from a good man is of value to me. What you hint at generally is very very true, that my work will be grievously hypothetical and large parts by no means worthy of being called inductive; my commonest error being probably induction from too few facts.

By his own admission, Darwin was using faulty generalizations, or what we would call "jumping to conclusions" to make his point. Thus, what Herschel called "speculative," Darwin called "grievously hypothetical" half a decade earlier and, perhaps, this is why Darwin could not raise any objections to Hershel's critique. It was because Darwin knew that Hershel was right, and he knew it several years before he published his book. In his response to Herschel, all Darwin could do was to appeal to popularity and authority, but one should question how serious Darwin was, as such an argument could have never convinced a man like Herschel. However, Darwin was right about one thing: his theory did, indeed, win in the long run.

As far as we can tell, Darwin's 1861 letter was the end of his correspondence with Herschel, although Herschel would live on for another decade. To Herschel, Darwin's theory was, perhaps, not worthy of more than a single footnote, but by influencing others, he contributed more to the birth of evolutionary biology than he would have ever wanted to take credit for. His other contributions to optics, astronomy, mathematics, geology, photography, chemistry, philosophy, and art—which are too many to enumerate in detail—are the accomplishments he would most likely want us to remember him for. Unfortunately for him, his opposition to Darwin was the main reason scholars have been interested in him for a long time. If, however, you ever visit Westminster Abbey, please take a little time to find Herschel's grave, where he has been resting since May 19, 1871, and pay your respects to this great man, whom we have forgotten for far too long. His gravestone should not be too hard to find. It is right next to Darwin's, who passed away a decade after him in 1882.

Chapter 2

Genesis of Genetics

The verification problem of Darwin's theory would not go away, but it would become less relevant over time. Heaps of speculation about a theory does not automatically falsify it as unfalsifiability is the very essence of a speculative theory. One cannot decide whether the claims of the theory are true or not, and so the decision becomes a question of preference. Speculative theories, owing to their very nature, can sometimes seem questionable or even provocative. Even so, just because someone agrees with a questionable theory does not mean they are wrong, and just because someone disagrees with it does not mean they are right. In the late nineteenth and the early twentieth century, science shifted away from its religious roots in natural theology and started viewing nature as a necessary premise for existence, with God as an unwanted guest in the story of the universe. The theory of evolution profoundly influenced the worldview of scientists, making naturalists less religious, but it is also possible that scientists started accepting evolution because their views had already changed by the time they started accepting it. Either way, God has been excommunicated from the sciences, and natural theology has become a thing of the past. One unfortunate consequence of the transition was the rebirth of religious fundamentalism, as many religious thinkers were less and less in favor of science. Fundamentalists criticized scientific thought for not acquiring knowledge from the revealed "holy" texts, which was, ironically, the same critique levied against natural theology half a century earlier. Conversely, the one thing going for the theory of evolution was that its principles, as Darwin predicted, had become far more acceptable in this new era than before. Despite a few lingering issues, such as Darwin's prior subscription to blending theory and Lamarckian inheritance, these were all swept away by the upheaval that the discovery of genetics brought, to the point that they are not worth discussing anymore.

In 1866, Gregor Mendel published his groundbreaking paper on plant hybridization, which was later recognized as the foundational work in the field of genetics, when several scientists verified Mendel's findings 34 years after they were published. Mendel, a monk with a passion for science, bred pea plants in the garden of his monastery and recorded several specific traits of these plants during his experiments to determine if any changes of those traits displayed a law-like characteristic. He, for example, bred plants that would always produce tall offspring and plants that would produce short offspring, then he crossbred these two and observed the resulting plants over several generations. He found that in the first generation of mixed-pea plants, all the new plants were tall, but in the second generation, three-fourths were tall, and one-fourth were short. Thus, a trait that disappeared in the first generation magically reappeared in the second, which at the time would have made anyone who believed that traits would blend in subsequent generations roll their eyes a little.

Mendel's explanation for this phenomenon was that every first-generation pea plant from the mixed breed had approximately one gene for short plants and one gene for tall plants, and because these genes overlapped each other, only the gene for tall plants was expressed. A gene in Mendelian genetics is simply a unit that stores an inheritable trait, such as color or size and so on. Sexually reproducing organisms generally inherit two versions of each gene, one from each parent. In the case of the first generation of the peas, one tall gene and one short was inherited from the ancestor plants, but the tall gene was dominant, which forced the plant to express it instead of the short gene. In the second generation, however, we also got plants that had two tall genes and two short genes, and not just the combination of the two. As each first-generation plant had one tall and one short gene, there was a fifty-fifty chance to inherit either, but only a 25% chance to inherit two short genes. Consequently, in the second generation, one-fourth of the plants had only a short gene, and one-fourth only had tall genes, while half of the plants had a mix of the two. As both the plants with two tall genes and the plants with one tall gene produced a tall plant, only the plants that had two short genes (approximately one-fourth of the whole population) produced short plants in the second generation.

Mendel's discovery meant that different specimens in the same group would, for the same attribute, possess different genes that were responsible for different traits. Each specimen in a group of plants possesses two sets of genes. In a single set, the gene responsible for a specific attribute, such as height, might be unique and singular, even though different specimens could possess different variations of that singular gene. For example, one plant can have the gene for the short trait or the gene for the tall trait in the same set, but not both. These sets of genes would eventually be called chromosomes. A single variation of a specific gene is called an allele. So, in the previous example, we spoke of a short allele and a tall allele of the gene responsible for the height attribute. Many genes have alternative versions; that is, many alleles of the same gene exist and are distributed across the same species. These alleles are responsible for the great variety of traits in populations we observe in nature. Different specimens can have a different makeup of gene variations or allele frequency, which might change over time as new generations adapt to their environment. This change can create new varieties of the same species and has been generally called the process of microevolution, but I will refer to it as genomic shuffling to avoid using language that would lead to prejudice. During genomic shuffling, the frequency of some alleles declines while the frequency of others surges in the same group, depending on environmental factors; so, the prevalence of each allele is constantly changing inside the population over subsequent generations owing to natural selection.

Mendel's laws of inheritance – although not recognized at the time – revealed that new variations could be effortlessly created without any prospect of creating new species. This might sound surprising, but without any further extension to Darwin's theory, Mendel's findings greatly diminish the prospects of evolution. Let's return to Mendel's experiment once more to see why this is the case. Let's say that we have a population of tall pea plants with yellow seed and white flowers, and we have another population of short pea plants with green seed and violet flowers. The traits of the first population are tall, yellow, and white, while those of the second are short, green, and violet. This means that we have three genes, and each gene has two alleles or, in other words, two variants. If we mix these two very specific plant populations, over time we will have pea plants that are tall with green seeds and violet flowers and pea plants that are short with yellow seeds and white flowers. We can create six new variants from the two we have started with, for a total of eight different pea plants. Depending on which alleles are dominant or recessive, the chance of a specific new variant's appearance might be higher or lower, but eventually we will have all eight variants, as long as we don't favor any trait over another. If we have three genes with two alleles each, we can create six new variants from only two. So, imagine what nature could do with thousands of genes and hundreds of alleles per gene if it needed to create a few more variants of a species. A seemingly infinite number of variants can be created by Mother Nature, if she desires it.

Thanks to Mendel and the first geneticists, it was no longer a mystery where the variation under domestication and nature that Darwin has observed had come from: it could be all explained by the law of inheritance and genomic shuffling. However, this posed a problem for Darwin's theory even though, at the time, not many scientists seemed to care. Natural selection was still assumed to be a major factor in selecting the traits that would be propagated over time; however, the laws of inheritance imposed strong limits on the variants that could appear as a result of genomic shuffling. It is true that the many genes of complex animals and plants had many alleles and could potentially produce billions upon billions of variants, but no such combination of alleles could ever create a new species. All alleles of all genes of a species are from the same species and can, therefore, produce nothing but the same species, no matter which combination of variants goes into creating a new generation. Even the most extreme cases of plant hybridization have these limits; even if you create every possible variant of a pea plant, not one of them could become something else but a pea plant. Much of the observable changes in nature, such as variation, could be explained by genomic shuffling, which is not the explanation Darwin had hoped for.

The Darwinists of the early twentieth century did not see any issue between the theory of evolution and Mendelian inheritance, yet we must not forget that the understanding of the limits of genetic variability at the time was not the same as it is today. For example, back in the day, you could believe that the genes necessary to make cats also existed inside dogs, only the cat alleles carried by dogs were less frequent and not combined in the same specimens as they were in cats. However, if you take the correct alleles from various breeds of dogs, perhaps you could create cats, and it wouldn't be a stretch to suppose that, perhaps, nature could not only do the same but had also done so in the past. There's nothing that would prevent someone from thinking this way, and, at the time, this would not have been a strange idea. In fact, this idea, which was referred to as the "views of the Weismann school" by Julian Huxley, is implicit in any theory of evolution based on pure Mendelian inheritance. It is only because of our more modern understanding of genes and genetics that we can avoid and disregard such ideas. It has been known for a while that most, perhaps even all, species have genes that are unique to them and, therefore, could not have been inherited in their current form from any ancestor or from any other being.

One of the three scientists who was instrumental in the establishment of genetics and is credited with coining the word "gene," was the Dutch botanist Hugo de Vries. He was an enthusiastic proponent of Darwin's theory, and came up, perhaps unwittingly, with a solution to the problem that the laws of inheritance posed to the theory of evolution. He proposed the idea of mutationism, which suggested that new traits could arise in an offspring over several generations that were not inherited from any of its ancestors. Vries believed that all species originated via mutations, which could, in theory, produce new novelties even over the lifetime of a single generation. Rather than a gradual change, as Darwin suggested, Vries believed that evolution would progress by leaps, thanks to the effects of mutations creating new attributes and traits. In 1901, he studied the evening primrose and discovered that sometimes completely new traits would appear in the wild plant population that Mendelian inheritance could not explain. These new traits were inheritable by new generations but were not present in earlier generations and, therefore, could not have been the result of genomic shuffling. He termed these changes "mutations," a word he might have gotten from Lyell's *Principles of Geology*, where it was used as a synonym for the sudden geological changes of the Earth's surface. Hugo de Vries believed that mutations were a common occurrence in nature and that they could create new forms of life more rapidly than the natural selection of variations could. Mutation theory was both a blessing and a curse for the Darwinian theory of evolution, as it opened a loophole in Mendel's theory, but it also stood in opposition to the gradualism that Darwin championed.

Further investigation of the mutationist theory exposed some flaws in the experiments de Vries used to prove the existence of mutations. One of the issues was that most of the mutations he had observed in primroses were actually chromosomal aberrations that rendered the plants infertile and, while the traits could be inherited, they would eventually disappear from the plant population. Another issue was that as a mutation was defined as the sudden appearance of a new characteristic absent from previous generations, changes in the gene frequency that created rare gene combinations could be potentially identified as a mutation. It would take some time before the first mutation we today would also call a mutation was observed in nature. Mutations could be easily produced and observed in test labs but finding them in nature proved to be an exceptionally difficult task. During this time, the theory of evolution shifted from the observation of plentiful variations easily found in nature to a desperate hunt for mutations. Even today, it is often quite difficult to find a genuine trait created by a mutation and perpetuated by natural selection.

In 1908, Thomas Hunt Morgan began his famous fruit fly experiments. He used several methods, such as radiation, to produce mutant flies in the lab. Most of these attempts ended in failure, but after a year, he discovered several mutations that could be inherited by the offspring of the mutated flies. Morgan and his students recorded the appearance of mutations over generations and discovered that some mutations, such as eye color and wing alterations, were somehow linked. Morgan speculated that the genes affected by the former mutations were genetically linked because they were located on the same chromosome and were, therefore, physically closer to each other than to other genes. The closer two genes were, the more likely they would be inherited together; this is why some seemingly unrelated mutations were also often inherited together. These discoveries eventually led Morgan to promote the idea of chromosomal crossovers.

The concept of chromosomal crossovers is an integral part of genetics. You might recall that complex living beings, such as animals and plants, inherit two sets of chromosomes from their parents, one chromosome from each. This system of inheritance looks simple until one realizes that the parents also have not one but two sets of chromosomes that they can give away, even though only one can be inherited by the offspring from each parent. The two parents together have four sets in total but pass along only two to their offspring. The question is simple: which set of chromosomes will the parent give to the offspring from the two it already owns? The answer is: neither and both at the same time. During chromosomal crossover, the chromosomes used for reproduction are created by combining each chromosome pair of the parent into one single chromosome, creating one set of chromosomes from the two existing ones. As the two original chromosome sets possessed two different alleles for every gene in them, only one of those alleles could be put into the new chromosomes. The alleles inherited are selected randomly; however, those that are physically closer to each other are more likely to be inherited together owing to a phenomenon called genetic linkage. Every single reproductive cell of an organism is different because each cell has a different combination of gene alleles mixed from the organism's own combined gene pool. No other cell in the organism's body possesses this particular combination of genes, and this is one of the reasons why offspring always look different when we compare them to either parent. Chromosomal crossover selects the gene variants that will be inherited by the offspring, but it also selects the ones that will not be inherited, so parents with few offspring might possess genes that will not be inherited by any of their offspring. Hence, some alleles might completely disappear from a population, potentially removing the traits associated with them from the group.

In Mendelian genetics, attributes and traits are directly related to genes and their alleles; however, the way biological creatures work is a bit more complicated than that. Instead of one gene being responsible for one attribute, in reality, one gene might affect several different attributes, and a single attribute might be affected by several different genes. Given how multipurpose genes are, the different combinations of alleles can produce specimens that look quite different from their ancestors only a few generations back. Such changes are largely responsible for the discrepancy between our domesticated plants and animals and their wild counterparts. Genomic shuffling, while limited in scope, can greatly affect the appearance and behavior of any species, but that should not be ever confused with the effects of mutations.

In 1959, the zoologist Dmitry Belyayev started experimenting on wild foxes to support Darwin's theory of evolution and Mendelian genetics with data. Belyayev bred foxes in captivity and selected the specimens that were the tamest and friendliest toward humans, essentially domesticating the species. The experiment produced remarkable results. After a few generations, foxes became much tamer and also acquired traits that were reminiscent of domesticated animals. For example, they started wagging their tails when humans approached. Many were born with floppy ears and rolled tails —traits typically associated with dogs and not foxes. Given how rare mutations are, it might be difficult to explain how these traits were acquired by simply mutating the species and selecting the desirable mutations over the less preferred ones. It would make more sense to suggest that these changes occurred because of genomic shuffling; in other words, thanks to the change in the allele frequency in the population. If these changes were in large part attributable to mutations, it would imply that the same mutations that happened in the chromosomes of foxes also happened in dogs, as both their outward appearance and behavior changed to be more like that of dogs. This would mean that not only, over a few generations, the species acquired beneficial mutations, but that they likely acquired the exact same beneficial mutations that other domesticated animals also had gained thousands of years ago.

It is also strange that we have a species that could be domesticated over a few generations, yet there are many other species that we have tried and failed to domesticate over the past 3000 years. If mutations can bring about domestic qualities in animals, why only these and not the others? It is a simple problem of numbers and probability. Genomic shuffling is a much simpler explanation than genetic mutation for most of the changes that Belyayev's foxes underwent.

Let's do a simple thought experiment. Let's say there's an elephant species living in a relatively hot environment and, in the population, there are ten genes each, with two alleles that control fitness related to temperature. Let's say that one gene is responsible for the length of the elephant's fur, and another for the amount of fat stored under the skin. We would have one allele for short fur and one for long, one for minimal fat, and one for lots of fat, and so on. As the animal is living in a hot temperature, the gene variants that favor the hot climate—such as short fur and minimal fat—are favored, so the more alleles adaptive to heat the animal has, the better. However, one or two cold climate-favoring alleles could still produce a viable specimen. Most elephants will have eight to ten hot alleles and zero to two cold alleles, but the cold alleles would be from the original ten cold alleles distributed equally in the population. Although this elephant population is geared toward surviving in hot weather, it still has alleles for surviving in cold weather. If the weather progressively shifts from hot to cold, the distribution of hot and cold alleles will also shift toward the prominence of cold alleles. If the temperature gets low enough, eventually, elephants with all ten cold alleles will be born, which would make them look very different from the elephants we started with. These new elephants could hypothetically look more like mammoths, even though the gene pool of the population would be no different from the gene pool before the temperature had changed. If found by modern humans, these elephants would most likely be categorized as a new species, even though there would be nothing new about them at all. Without extensive analysis of the genome, it is impossible to differentiate new variants from mutations, and one is easily mistaken for the other. Given this, how would we be able to discover if such a thing had happened in the not-so-distant past?

During his voyage, Darwin came across several different birds on the Galapagos Islands. These birds would be later aptly called Darwin's finches and were believed to belong to 12 different groups of distinct species at the time of their discovery. They seemed to be a textbook example of evolutionary change, as each species looked different and was uniquely adapted to the environment, depending on which island of the Galapagos they came from. In particular, the size and shape of their beaks looked very distinct from one another, which is why these birds were categorized as belonging to different groups of species. This has not changed, even though almost all of them have been observed to mate with finches from the other groups, and their genetic analysis has proven this to be a common occurrence in the past, and their genetic makeup was extremely mixed. Today, these finches are still officially considered as belonging to different species, and their mating is still called hybridization, even though their offspring are just as fertile as their ancestors. Darwin himself highlighted in the *Origin* that it was extremely challenging for naturalists to distinguish species from subspecies and noted that their methods were often very ad hoc, which would lead to confusion where one naturalist would categorize an animal as a species, and another as a subspecies. Perhaps, this is what happened in the case of Darwin's finches. It is possible that they are all subspecies of the same species and don't belong to different species groups; but, even if that is not the case, it cannot be disputed that all their variations in physical appearance can be simply explained by the genomic shuffling of the finch gene alleles in the Galapagos.

The rise of mutationism was not the only issue Darwin's theory faced in the early twentieth century. Many have criticized the lack of rigor in evolutionary thought. The theory was just as speculative as any other hypothesis before Darwin's, and nothing has changed since in this regard. The idea certainly had its own appeal, and the theory gained a large following in the English-speaking world, but outside, it was still viewed with suspicion and disbelief. This disbelief gave birth to several critics, whose arguments found their way back to Britain and caused discord in the birthplace of the theory. The task to save the theory from a slow death fell to the British statistician Ronald A. Fischer, who formulated several evolutionary concepts into mathematical equations. This allowed for a more scientific approach to address criticisms, but it also increased the barrier of entry to the field, as not everyone could understand the mathematics Fischer used. Even today, the meaning, application, and validity of Fischer's main contribution to the theory, the "fundamental theorem of natural selection," remains the object of some debate. Sewall Wright, an American geneticist, had a similar idea called the "adaptive landscape" that is often cited to this day, but, at the time, Fischer's work was considered more mainstream. Both concepts were included in Julian Huxley's *Evolution: The Modern Synthesis*, which became the cornerstone of a new theory.

Huxley took the evolutionary ideas of the previous 40 years and put them in the same book, integrating theories from different people into one overarching hypothesis, which has been named "neo-Darwinian synthesis." This was the birth of neo-Darwinism, and, in many respects, this is when the modern theory of evolution, as we understand it today, was born. Many of the founders of these ideas did not necessarily agree, and yet that didn't stop Huxley to put all their ideas into one comprehensive, unifying book. His book was more readable compared with Fischer's, and, so, it was also more popular. To the casual observer, it must have seemed that the problems of Darwinian thought were either already solved or were in the process of being solved. However, this was not the case. Both Fischer and Sewall based their theory on the concept of fitness, and the adequacy of fitness to explain evolution is questionable, at best. There's a reason why Fischer named his equation the "fundamental theorem of natural selection" and not "the fundamental theorem of evolution."

Fischer's theorem claims that the fitness of a population increases as natural selection alters the gene frequency of alleles inside a population. This, in general, is true, of course. The adaptive landscape of Sewall adds that occasionally fitness decreases before it can increase and, thus, it is not a continuous ascension, but rather one with many obstacles. This is technically true, depending on what type of interpretation you use for fitness. For example, if the environment of a species changes, then the population's genetic makeup must also change before it can ascend to a new peak of fitness in the same adaptive landscape. Depending on your definition of fitness, you may see this as a single ascent or an alternating climb and descent. The population on the top of the previous peak and at the bottom of that peak is the exact same species without alterations, so suggesting that fitness is lost when only the environment changes does not necessarily make sense. Either way, both Fischer and Sewall were only concerned with natural selection and the fact that it increased fitness in subsequent generations, which is generally and fundamentally true. This was not in dispute neither before nor after Darwin, but the fact that these two created a mathematical framework for testing this claim was a worthwhile addition to the science of biology. The problem is that they did not prove anything that was not already known or accepted. Darwin simply framed his process in terms of variability, while they framed it in terms of fitness. It is the exact same book, with a slightly different cover. Just as Darwin established the law of variation, so did Fischer establish the law of fitness and, the same way Darwin's law of higgledy-piggledy was inadequate to explain speciation, so was Fischer's. Neither proposed a law of speciation; therefore, neither can prove nor disprove the theory of evolution. Fitness increasing in a population is not evidence that this process will, over time, create a new species. It might, but the change in fitness alone can't prove that. Natural selection can change the variability of gene alleles in a species until the end of time, and yet not change the species into another species. What might have happened, or what might not have happened, is not something science is generally interested in. As far as science is concerned, anything is possible. The question is always what is more likely and what is less likely to happen or have happened and not anything else. We need a fundamental theorem of evolution and not anything else.

The modern synthesis brought the theory to its current state. Details of the theory altered with time, but the fundamentals stayed the same. The neo-Darwinian theory is straightforward and easy to understand. While it is true that genomic shuffling limits the variability of a species, the effects of mutations could always create new genes and new alleles of existing genes. This would break the chain that inheritance forces upon the species and could potentially lead to new forms of life. Natural selection acts both on the many variations of genes in a population, and the new genes and alleles mutations create at the same time. If a mutation is positive or neutral in terms of its effect on the fitness of the population, then the mutation itself is likely to survive and propagate. Over the generations, these mutations can accumulate in the genome and could potentially divide the species into groups that would evolve into a new and distinct species. Even if all of this is eventually proven to be true, at the moment, the theory is hopelessly speculative. The likelihood of a mutation propagating is low, and the chance of it surviving and also contributing to speciation is even lower. There's a fight for survival in nature, and any new mutation in a gene must not only compete with the overwhelming dominance of the preexisting alleles but also with the possible mixes of those alleles. If the mutation does not provide a significant advantage to the species, it will be weeded out by natural selection, and the greater the effect the mutation has on the specimen, the less likely the effect will be positive. Many organs of the animal body are very delicate and could not have been created by large intrusive mutations, but only via small ones, which are less likely to persist to begin with. Even if these small mutations persevere, what is the likelihood that there's a path of sequential mutations of limited size to reach an organ, such as the heart, brain, lungs, and so on, at the end of the path? All of that is assumed: that small mutations can accumulate into something more complex with a definite purpose or function. Evolution may work exactly as described and the many forms of life may have descended from one another. However, to suggest that the theory of evolution has proven this, is just a pretense of knowledge, no different from a belief in creationism or the centuries-old notion that the earth is flat.

The idea that the earth is flat has become a symbol of the Dark Ages, a sign of the intellectual deficiencies of a less-advanced culture than ours. We may justifiably ridicule today's Flat Earthers for believing in something despite the overwhelming evidence to the contrary. Many forget that, if we lived in the early Middle Ages, there may have not been that many reasons to doubt that the Earth was flat. In fact, if we ourselves were living in the fourth century, we might have also believed that the Earth was flat. And why wouldn't we have? To the casual observer, the Earth seems flat, and why would anyone test for the possibility of the Earth being spherical or something different if we already had a practical theory accepted by most people? What we see today and what people saw back then is fundamentally the same and, unless a person is purposely looking for the small anomalies that imply the spherical form, one won't take issue with the flat-Earth hypothesis. Therefore, if a scholar in the fourth century would have said that "the Earth is most likely flat" that would have been his honest opinion, based on the facts he had available at that time. Would he have been justified in his belief, as long as evidence contrary to it was not available to him? Was the theory of the flat Earth bad only after it was discovered to be false, or was it always bad, and people just didn't realize that, and would it have been fine as long as it had turned out to be correct? Would being accidentally correct have changed things, even if the theory was the same as the one we ridicule today? It should have been clear even back then that the requirements for a well-established theory were not met by the flat-Earth hypothesis. It should have been clear as day for anyone willing and capable of verifying its validity. Even so, many people from ancient times chose to not doubt the theory and, knowing this, can we say with confidence that the theory of evolution is different in this regard? There is fundamentally nothing wrong in believing evolution; however, calling it a fact or a well-established science might be a bit of a stretch, unless a well-formulated argument backed by credible and relevant evidence is presented that verifies its various claims and predictions. If we lack such evidence, however, we may not be better than the ancient scholar who believed that the Earth was flat, even if we are willing to entertain the possibility that we are wrong and are willing to consider the evidence that may prove us wrong.

Chapter 3

Biology of Molecules

In the second part of the twentieth century, a brand-new chapter on the science of molecular biology was written owing to the discovery of the structure of DNA. DNA is the molecule inside our cells that contains all of our genes, and it was hoped that understanding DNA would finally answer the great questions of life's origin, but it seems to have created as many questions as it has answered. DNA is the chemical equivalent of the chromosomes discovered during the early days of genetics. Understanding the structure of DNA played a pivotal role in revealing the particular mechanisms behind gene expression and genetic inheritance. Advancements in molecular biology revealed the almost uniform genetic code and the cause and nature of genetic mutations. This progress had a dramatic effect on our lives, as it led to the creation of new medicines and genetically modified organisms (GMOs), but it did not alter the modern theory of evolution considerably. Our understanding of the specific mechanisms may have expanded significantly, but that did not lead to any radical changes in the fundamentals of the theory. While these discoveries in molecular biology did not cause any upheavals for the theory, they did reveal an issue not directly related to evolution but still significant in its own right and problematic to it.

When Darwin first conceived his theory, it was clear to him that evolution could not have been responsible for the existence of every single living being that has ever existed because evolution could only begin after life was already in existence. He believed there had to be some "patient zero" from which all other species had to have descended. While the existence of bacteria had been extensively accepted by the time Darwin's book came out, it was only during its first publication that the idea that bacteria spontaneously create itself from matter was finally disproven. During the next hundred years, it was firmly established that both multicellular organisms and simple bacteria are made primarily from proteins, which in turn are made from a select few amino acid variants. The origin of life studies primarily concentrated on amino acids and their origins, as DNA had not yet been discovered. The prevailing theory was that the amino acids required for the first organism were created by chemical reactions, sometimes referred to as chemical evolution, and once the first organism was created, it would kick-start the biological evolution of living beings. This idea, dubbed abiogenesis by Thomas Huxley, is the opposite of the ancient idea that proposed that all life originated from other life and that inanimate matter could not be brought to life. Huxley referred to the earlier idea of life's infinite regression as biogenesis and the opposite, of life beginning from matter, abiogenesis.

Abiogenesis seemed to be a promising idea in the twentieth century. In 1952, Stanley L. Miller and Harold C. Urey conducted an experiment in which they mixed, heated, and electrocuted several gases inside sealed flasks. They managed to create, among other things, several amino acids that were known to be essential to the construction of proteins. At the time, this was considered a great success in the field of origin of life studies, and it is, to this day, the most famous experiment that was conducted to better understand abiogenesis. The reason this experiment is considered the greatest in the field is that, after this test, research ground to a halt and no meaningful results were produced for decades. Even the value of the Miller–Urey experiment has been greatly reduced, as the basic assumptions behind the test are no longer accepted in science. The same year that the Miller experiment was conducted, Alfred Hershey and Martha Chase did an experiment that once and for all proved that DNA, or nucleic acids, and not amino acids were the carriers of the genetic material responsible for inheritance. A year later, Watson and Crick published their discovery regarding the structure of DNA, captivating the world with the now-iconic form of the double helix. These advancements in molecular biology and the numerous discoveries that followed were also ultimately responsible for the stagnation of experimental research in the origin of life studies. The field of molecular biology became so complicated that it was simply too difficult to create a new hypothesis that could account for every known fact and still be considered realistic.

Many theories sprung up since the Miller–Urey experiment, but because abiogenesis does not require millions of years to progress, any theory that could not be verified by experiment had difficulty in getting accepted. Many hoped that understanding the cell chemistry would reveal the secret origins of life, but what really happened was the exact opposite of what they had hoped for. It made it almost impossible to even conceive how life could have first originated from the inanimate matter because of the difficulties associated with the synthetization of even the simplest single-celled organism known to man. Some of these problems are chemical. The necessary conditions to create the many chemical elements needed to create the basic molecules can be quite diverse, and some molecules are difficult to keep together while others are difficult to keep away from molecules that would destroy them. The machinery of the cell does a great job of preventing the molecules inside the cell wall from destroying or bonding prematurely with each other, but without preventative measures, it becomes a bonding free-for-all for the acidic molecules that destroys their usefulness. This is one of the problems that has not yet been solved. Another problem is more subtle. You could call it a statistical problem. To be able to understand this problem, we need to dig deeper into the mechanisms that make life function and survive in a fundamentally hostile world. This part will be much more detailed than a layman would normally wish for, but I believe, it is imperative that we understand how life on a basic level works if we are to discuss its origin and mysteries. I also believe that molecular biology is a fascinating subject that most documentaries don't represent in sufficient detail, robbing people of the joy of understanding how life on a fundamental level looks and behaves.

There are two functions a single-celled organism must fulfill: survival and reproduction. To facilitate these functions, it must be able to create the molecules it needs to survive and conserve and replicate the information necessary to make these required molecules. The first is accomplished by the process of protein synthesis and the second by DNA replication. Protein synthesis is, in general, the process by which the information located in the genes of DNA is translated from a sequence of nucleobases to a sequence of amino acids, which are then assembled into a protein. The prerequisite to make this process happen is the presence of a DNA strand that contains a series of nucleobases with the correct sequence to create the amino acid chain of a specific protein. The chemical structure of DNA is a double helix built from two strands, each made of a phosphate backbone on the outside to which a sequence of nucleobases is attached on the inside. The strands are connected through hydrogen bonds of individual nucleobases, meaning that they are connected on the inside of the molecule, right where the information is being stored. DNA is often referred to as a double-stranded molecule because of the two phosphate backbones and the two series of nucleobases that connect the two strands. For example, RNA, which is another molecule the cell uses, generally has only one backbone and one sequence of bases attached to it and is, therefore, not double-stranded. In DNA, each strand is a sort of mirror image of the other, and, therefore, both strands contain the exact same information. One strand will always be inverted compared with the strand that is responsible for producing proteins, the same way an image seen in a mirror is inverted compared with reality.

It might be difficult to imagine the composition of DNA or understand the implications of its design from such a short description; perhaps, the next example will help in revealing the remarkable features hidden in its structure. Imagine a book on a table, preferably a long one with a hard cover, such as *War and Peace*. Now imagine that the front and back covers are removed, and the pages are only held in place by the spine of the book. If this book were one of the strands of the double helix, the spine would be the phosphate backbone of the strand, and each individual page would be equal to a single nucleobase. To build DNA, we need the other strand of the double helix as well, so we need another copy of the same book, and we need to remove the covers from this one as well, leaving the spine intact once again. The next step is to put the book on the table right next to the first one. Now imagine that you rotate the second book on the table by 180°, so that the paper ends are facing each other and the spines are facing away from each other; this would mean that the text in one book would be upside down, which is okay, as we have no intention to read from the second book. What you need to do next is to push these two books into each other with every other page overlapping, like you would with two stacks of cards. This means that, after one page of the first book, you will always see a page from the second book and after that, another page from the first book and so on. Subsequently, you will have these alternating pages from two books, and to make this thing even harder to open, you need to glue every set of alternating two pages together. You never glue more than two pages, and you never glue a page from a book to another page from the same book. You only glue a page from one book to a page from the other book. Once that is accomplished, you will have two spines—phosphate bones—on the outside with two sets of pages—nucleobases—attached, which are also glued together on the inside with paper glue—hydrogen bonds. In other words, you have DNA. The only structural difference between this hypothetical mess and DNA is that the double strands of DNA look much more like two spiral stairs running in parallel, rather than the rigid and linear spines of two books interlaced with one another.

It should be obvious that trying to read information from DNA is not a simple feat, as all the nucleobases are locked tightly in the center of the molecule. This might seem strange at first but, if you think about it, there is a reason for this rigidity. If DNA was single-stranded, it would contain the exact same amount of information as it does now. That is a fact. However, if the other strand went missing, then all the hydrogen bonds would also disappear, and that would mean that every nucleobase that still remains would be quick to interact with other molecules to form new hydrogen bonds, making any other kind of subsequent interaction impossible. Even if no other molecule was present to take advantage of the missing hydrogen bonds, DNA could easily curl and connect different parts of its own nucleobases together; this could ruin DNA and stop it from being functional. Any long-term storage of information, be it biomechanical or digital, must have a solution for this problem. A storage unit has to be able to interact with the outside so that the outside can access the information stored inside. Simultaneously, it has to lock out the outside so it will not destroy the information inside via the process of reading or by using a different kind of interaction.

In our cell, nucleobases carry genetic information, and in the case of DNA, when we talk about bases, we are always referring to nucleobase pairs that are glued together by hydrogen bonds. There are only four bases in DNA, but any gene on one strand could potentially have any combination of those four in its sequence. The bases are (A)denine, (T)hymine, (C)ytosine, and (G)uanine. You can think of them as the biological equivalent of the digital world's zeroes and ones, except that, instead of having the two binary states o and I in DNA, we have four states: A, T, C, and G. The whole sequence of nucleobases inside a DNA strand is made from these four bases. There's one major difference between the bases of DNA and the binary data of computers. Bases are all paired with another specific base, and I don't mean just chemically, but on a fundamental structural level as well. You see, adenine and thymine each can only form two hydrogen bonds total, but cytosine and guanine can form three, so adenine will always form a bond with thymine, and cytosine with guanine and vice versa. Thus, if on one strand of DNA we have the sequence AATTCCGG, on the parallel strand, we would find TTAAGGCC, owing to the effects of the structural pairing. Similar to how our first book's pages were glued to their upside-down counterpart in the second book, so too do the bases of a strand get attached to their complementary base located on the other strand.

It is crucial that we memorize the bases and their pairings, or the letters TACG and the pairings of T–A and C–G. The easiest way to remember the pairings for me was to simply memorize CG together as CG is an abbreviation of Computer Graphics, which is commonly used in reference to visual effects in movies created with the use of computers. Why life uses this four-base-double-pairing system is not important for the moment. What's important is that the sequence of bases found on one strand is not the same as the sequence on the other one. They are similar, but not the same. The strands are reflections of one another, as if a mirror had been placed alongside one strand and the other one was made based on the mirror image. From the standpoint of computer science, they are equal because they store the same information content, but from a biochemical viewpoint, they are quite different because their function is not the same.

During the first phase of protein synthesis, an enzyme called RNA polymerase attaches itself to a section of DNA (promoter) and breaks the hydrogen bonds that connect the two strands. After this, the RNA polymerase starts adding nucleobases to the free bases on one of the strands, called the template strand. The template strand's nucleobases that are freed from their hydrogen bonds by RNA polymerase are connected to a newly formed sequence of bases (created by the RNAP), which contain a complementary sequence of bases relative to the template strand. During this process, the other strand does nothing, but because it contains the same sequence of bases as the molecule being formed, it is called the coding strand. Once the whole gene has been processed by the RNA polymerase into nucleobases, the new strand is detached from the template strand. This new strand, which is only a fraction of length that of DNA, is called messenger RNA. Unlike DNA, it has only one strand instead of two, but other than that, it is generally the same kind of molecule. RNA has a phosphate backbone, and the nucleobases are connected to it just like in DNA. One notable difference is that it uses an altered and less stable form of thymine, which is called (U)racil, so, in messenger RNA, the base adenine is paired to uracil instead of thymine. The step that creates an RNA copy of a gene located on the template strand is called the process of transcription. Essentially, a part of DNA gets transcribed into an RNA molecule.

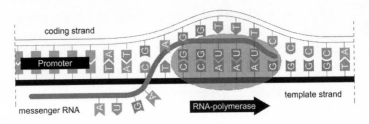

Transcription

If you want to understand the role and function of messenger RNA, think of it as the short-term memory of the cell. When you see something or learn something, it will be eventually stored in your long-term memory, which is difficult to access, just like DNA. Long-term memory stores lots of information, so capacity is more crucial than availability. It takes effort to recall a specific memory; however, once a memory is put from your long-term memory into your short-term memory, it becomes readily available for a short duration. The same is true for DNA and messenger RNA. DNA is the long-term memory of the cell and, when a specific part of memory is needed, it will be transcribed into messenger RNA, in other words into the short-term memory of the cell. Once the messenger RNA is created, it is available for use by the cell for a short duration, just as short-term memory tends to be preserved for a little while, but eventually, it breaks apart until it is recalled from DNA once again.

Gene expression, in general, starts with the process of transcription. However, as not all genes code for proteins, the second step of protein synthesis does not take place for all genes that are expressed. Some messenger RNAs have a different function and are, therefore, not used directly in protein synthesis. However, the messenger RNAs created from genes that code for proteins naturally initiate the second step, in which the sequence of nucleobases of the messenger RNA must be translated to a sequence of amino acids to form a new protein. This step is called translation, and while translating between these molecules sounds simple, there's a bit of a problem that complicates things. While there are four types of bases (TCAG), proteins are made of roughly 20 amino acids. That is, a single base cannot be translated into one amino acid because that would limit the kinds of amino acids that could be put into an amino acid chain to four, instead of the 20 that proteins are made from. A protein can contain hundreds of amino acids, but each of those must be from a set of 20 or so amino acids. A sequence of bases could potentially encode a sequence of amino acids, but only if an amino acid was defined by more than a single nucleobase. With one base you can encode four amino acids, but with two bases, you can encode 16 amino acids. Sixteen is still not sufficient to encode all of the 20 amino acids, but with three bases, 64 amino acids could be encoded. Hence, every amino acid in a protein-coding gene is defined by exactly three bases. The sequence of three bases is a fundamental unit in the genetic code called a codon.

The genetic code is a code table that pairs codons and amino acids. For example, the codon CTT matches the amino acid leucine. Except for the stop codon, all codons match a single amino acid. The stop codon is a special codon that signals the end of an amino acid chain and does not match any of the amino acids. You can think of the genetic code as being like Morse code, except that, instead of matching dots and dashes with letters, it matches a sequence of bases to amino acids. One key difference is that the sequence length of the Morse code varies between characters. For example, the letter A is represented by dot–dash while the letter Q is dash–dash–dot–dash. Therefore, a Morse character can be represented by two or even four signal characters, which differs from the genetic code's reliance on the fundamental unit of a codon being three bases long. This aspect of the genetic code resembles code made for computers more than natural language or anything else made by humans.

The old ASCII code, which was a standard that defined how binary numbers and the English alphabet were matched, also used a fixed-sequence length. Originally, this length was seven, so, for example, the binary representation of the letter A was 1000001 and representation of the letter Q was 1010001, and so on. Using seven binary characters, or seven bits, we can define 128 characters, exactly twice as many as the genetic code can encode with one codon, which is only 64. Now obviously, you don't need 128 coding characters to represent every character in the English alphabet, but if you added them all up: 26 lower-case plus 26 upper-case letters, plus 10 numbers, then you already filled 62 positions. If, instead of seven binary bits, we wanted to use only six, we would have 64 positions, but, with the 62 already taken, we would only have two left for every punctuation mark, which would be insufficient. With seven binary bits, every punctuation mark can be represented and more; but, with fewer bits, it is simply not feasible to do so. This is similar to the genetic code and its 20 amino acids that couldn't fit on two bases because two bases could only code for 16 amino acids, which is not adequate. In the case of seven-bit ASCII, even with every punctuation mark defined, there is plenty of room left for other characters to be coded, so you might wonder, what was the extra space used for? A large segment of it was used to define control characters, 33 to be exact. These control characters were originally designed to code for instructions that the computer could receive and interpret; however, owing to the changing technology, most of them became deprecated so are no longer in use. During the 1960s, when ASCII codes were developed, some text-based file systems could determine the end of a file using a special control character that signaled the location to the operating system. This character is called the End Of File (or EOF) character, and, in ASCII, it was defined as the number 011010. In some places, this character is still used even today. The concept of the EOF character is similar to the stop codon of genes, and the reason for their existence is also very similar. Neither old computers nor the cell knows in advance where the end of a file or a gene resides and, therefore, would not know where to stop the reading process without the EOF or stop codon.

If you recall that the genetic code codes for 20 amino acids plus the stop codon, while a codon can code 64 states, then you might wonder what the genetic code uses the remaining 42 slots for? In the ASCII code, the remaining space was used for control and rare Latin characters, but the genetic code is different. The genetic code does not code anything else than the 21 codons mentioned before. Thus, is the extra space made up of unused slots so that when new amino acids are required by a not yet existing, living being, they could be filled? Not quite. You see, the genetic code is rather unique, in that multiple codons may code for the same object, in this case for the same amino acid. For example, the amino acid leucine is coded by the codons TTA, TTG, CTT, CTC, CTA, and CTG, so six codons in total. Even the stop codon is defined by three specific codons, namely TAA, TAG, and TGA; this feature of the code that makes the amino acids overloaded is commonly referred to as the degeneracy of the genetic code. Different amino acids are coded by several different codons, from as few as one to as much as six, and the end result is that all 64 codons do, in fact, code for something. There's no empty space in the genetic code, so there is no room for new amino acids in it. It is not known for certain why the genetic code is set up the way it is, but it is strongly believed it is because of a side effect of molecular life: the threat of mutations.

Whenever DNA is accessed by the cell for any reason, or when the DNA molecule interacts with radiation or harmful chemicals, there's a potential risk that DNA will be damaged. This damage can be repaired by the molecular machinery of the cell; however, the success of the repair strongly depends on the extent of the damage. Sometimes recovery is too difficult or the machinery that repairs DNA isn't sufficient. In such cases, repaired DNA may not be identical to the original DNA in terms of its nucleobase sequence. Viral infections can also change DNA. If the sequence of bases in the DNA of a protein-coding gene is altered, it will also most likely alter the bases in the messenger RNA used to construct the correct protein. This would imply that the amino acid chain that the messenger RNA is translated into might have a different amino acid or amino acids somewhere in the chain, which could potentially alter the function of the protein. Excluding viral mutations, all mutations fall into a few simple categories such as duplication, shift, and point mutation. The most common of these is point mutation, which results in a single base being replaced by one of the other three possible nucleobases, and this could cause a change in the amino acid chain, where one specific amino acid would be replaced by a different one. For example, if the last base in the codon TTA changes into a T, transforming the codon to TTT, then the amino acid in the chain marked by that codon changes from leucine to phenylalanine. On the other hand, if the last base changes into a G, then the amino acid does not change, as both TTA and TTG code for leucine. The genetic code is not arranged randomly. The same amino acids are coded by codons that are very similar to each other in their arrangement of bases; so, if a mutation happens, there's a modest probability, depending on the codon's prominence in the code, that it will have little or no effect on the sequence of the amino acid chain. There are even cases when a specific point mutation can't alter the protein's basic structure at all. For example, if the last base in CTT changes, it will not change leucine to anything else because CTT, CTC, CTA, and CTG all code the same amino acid. Minimizing the effects of mutations is most likely the primary reason for the genetic code's overzealous matching of different codons to the same amino acids.

If we return to the second phase of protein synthesis, where the actual matching happens, we see that the structural pairing between specific nucleobases plays a vital role in the process of translation. When the messenger RNA needs to get translated into a protein, a complex molecular machine called the ribosome attaches itself to the messenger RNA strand. Once attached, the ribosome starts moving along the strand, processing the codons individually and building an amino acid chain in the process. Each codon in the messenger RNA is matched with a molecule known as a transfer RNA, an RNA codon with an amino acid attached to it. When the right type of transfer RNA enters, the ribosome removes the amino acid from the transfer RNA and adds it to the growing amino acid chain. Each transfer RNA contains an anticodon, a codon with the expressed purpose of matching another codon.

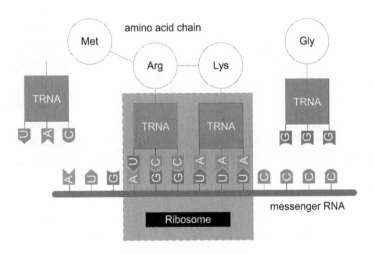

Translation

The cell has many transfer RNAs, prepared in advance with many different anticodons and attached amino acids. Some of the anticodons take advantage of the fact that the codons that define the same amino acid are located close to each other on the genetic code. The first two bases of the anti-codon work as expected, so adenine is matched with uracil and guanine with cytosine. In RNA, thymine is replaced by uracil and, although T and U are different, as a unit of information, they are equivalent. The third base of the transfer RNA behaves differently from the first two, which follows the strict matching rules we discussed before. The third base can create a wobble-base pair; that is, some of the bases on the anticodon's third position can pair with multiple different bases, rather than just the one it is normally associated with. For example, uracil can pair with both adenine and guanine when it is found on the third base of the anticodon. Some unconventional nucleobases may also be found at that location, such as hypoxanthine, which can pair with all the bases except guanine; in other words, it can pair not just with two, but three bases in total. The resulting wobbling base-pair provides a clever way for the cell to take advantage of the degeneracy of the genetic code, which would have been unnecessary if every amino acid was defined by no more than a single codon.

Every time a codon of the messenger RNA inside the ribosome is matched with an anticodon of a transfer RNA, a new amino acid is added to the growing amino acid chain. This process is similar to how radio operators interpret messages in Morse over the radio. Every time a radio operator recognizes a unit of Morse code, he adds a letter to the paper in front of him, writing the message letter by letter. Only when the final letter is added to the paper is the message complete. In the case of the cell, it is the protein that is being completed one amino acid at a time instead of a letter. Once the protein is completed, some additional changes might be required to make it completely functional; but, basically, protein synthesis stops once the last codon of the messenger RNA is matched and the ribosome reaches the stop codon. The messenger RNA repeats this process over and over until it is broken apart by the cell or until it decays naturally. Proteins are crucial because they are used to make most of the cell's machinery; even the ribosome that is responsible for creating proteins is made from roughly 50 protein molecules and a few RNA molecules.

DNA plays a key role in protein synthesis as the device that stores the information for all the proteins needed to make a cell. Therefore, when the cell divides, it is crucial that the whole DNA strand gets replicated along with the rest of the cell. Other parts of the organism are simple to replicate because they can be created following the genetic procedures stored in DNA, but DNA replication itself requires its unique apparatus, owing to the molecule's large size and delicate nature. The process of DNA replication is carried out by multiple proteins. It is a rather complicated process, which involves many enzymes, the most important probably the DNA helicase. It attaches to the DNA strand in different places and breaks the hydrogen bonds that connect the two strands of DNA. Two helicases are attached at roughly the same spot and move along the strands in opposite directions, separating the two strands in both directions like two sliders on the same zipper moving opposite to each other. This allows the DNA polymerase enzymes to attach themselves to both separated strands and add the complementary bases and a new phosphate backbone to the individual strands as they move along them up and down.

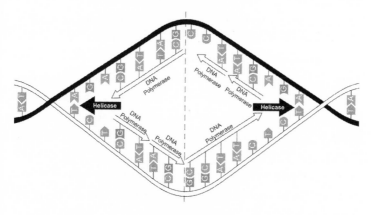

DNA Replication

Unfortunately, the phosphate backbone of DNA is only symmetrical in the opposite direction and DNA polymerase cannot move along on both strands indefinitely in the same direction. While on one strand, a single DNA polymerase can follow the helicase indefinitely, on the other strand, multiple DNA polymerases are needed to attach and detach themselves from the strand, and they can only complete minor segments of DNA every time they do so. The former strand is called the leading strand, while the latter is called the lagging strand because it lags behind the leading one. Owing to this asymmetrical construction, the DNA formed from the lagging strand takes more time to complete. This is a minor but important complication during DNA replication, as it makes the process somewhat harder to achieve because all these DNA fragments created on the lagging strands also need to be connected once the DNA polymerases finish creating them.

Note that while the whole process starts at multiple sites on the DNA strand as the machines work and complete their tasks, they will naturally crawl closer to each other as a result. Once the whole process is finished, if everything goes well, we will have two identical DNA strands. As both the coding strand and the template strand are complementary to each other, if the two are separated, and a new strand is added to both, the result must be two new double-stranded DNA molecules that contain the exact same order of their nucleobase pairs. Unfortunately, no system is perfect, and sometimes an error happens during DNA replication that could alter the original base sequence of DNA. Such mutation happens once every 10 million base pairs and may be fixed by the cell, depending on the complexity of the organism in question. This error-detecting feature could potentially further reduce the error rate to one-in-a-billion base pairs.

In a regular DNA molecule, both strands contain the whole genome; therefore, both strands can be used to create perfectly functional double-stranded DNA. This is what DNA replication takes advantage of by supplementing both strands with a new complementary strand at the exact same time. We have to recognize that DNA is a strange storage device because it contains the same information twice. Both the template strand and the coding strand contain the exact same sequence of units of information even though the coding strand has no function in gene expression and is only useful during replication. The cell could function without the coding strand, as its only purpose is to keep the template strand intact by stopping it from making hydrogen bonds with other molecules. While the coding strand does fulfill this goal, there are easier ways to accomplish this than inverting and duplicating the entire genome. For example, if the wobbling nucleobase hypoxanthine could form bonds with itself, and not just the other three bases, then it could not only replace guanine in the template strand but also replace all bases on the coding strand, simplifying the whole DNA molecule. Even if this replacement only worked in theory, it's hard to imagine that there's no alternative solution that would achieve the same result, given the versatility of chemicals found inside every cell. It should be a far easier task to construct a coding strand that is uniform, instead of one that is the inverse of the template strand.

So, why is it that the coding strand exists and takes the particular form of an inverted duplicate of the other strand? Why does DNA have this data duplication that seems so fundamental to its structure? No storage technology works like that in modern computers, at least not by design. You might think that the second copy of any information could be used as a backup, and that is somewhat true, but, in this particular case, that suggestion makes little sense. As the two strands are inverted, the data they contain on both strands are found at the exact same base location. Any damage that is caused on one strand is likely to harm the other strand, and because the backup is located at the same place, there's a good chance that both the information on the template strand and the same information on the coding strand will be lost. It is important to not keep your backup in the same place as you keep your original data; else, there's a good chance you lose both when something goes wrong, which defeats the purpose of having a backup. Of course, if one strand survives, the cell can use it to fix the other strand, but that is not the reason why data are duplicated in DNA. If the cell wanted to have a backup, it would make more sense to keep a copy of the whole DNA. For example, sexually reproducing organisms have two chromosomes, rather than one, fulfilling the same purpose. Moreover, multicellular organisms can have billions of cells, each with their own DNA, and simple organisms, like bacteria, make copies of themselves, including their own DNA, which is probably the best possible backup anyone can think of.

The reason DNA is constructed this way is simply that this structure makes it really easy to make copies of itself from itself. When the cell divides, one cell gets the DNA created from the template strand and the other cell gets the DNA created from the coding strand. If our coding strand was uniform rather than the inverse of the template strand, then every time the cell divided, it would have to create a proper coding strand just so a second template strand could be made from it. After that, this coding strand would become useless until the next cell division, so it makes sense to keep it intact as a part of DNA, instead of destroying it. This structure is exceptional as no modern computer hardware storing information can be replicated as easily as DNA can be. We can make copies of our data rapidly true, but that is because our computers replicate data electronically and not physically. This allows us to make quick copies of anything, but only if we have the storage capacity for those copies. Accordingly, we keep untold amounts of storage empty so that it could be used when necessary, while the cell creates storage on demand when it replicates DNA and wastes none whatsoever.

What needs to be recognized regarding DNA is that its structure on a fundamental structural level supports the process of replication. If DNA did not have both strands, it could not be replicated so easily. Moreover, if the nucleobases could not be paired A to T and C to G, then DNA would not have a coding strand, and so conventional replication would not work. In theory, we could have less bases in DNA, but they would still need to be paired if we wanted to make a coding strand. All amino acids could be defined using three bases instead of four using the same three-base codon length, making the system simpler, but then the bases could not be paired, and there would be no coding strand unless one base was able to pair with itself. The complex structure of DNA seems to purposefully facilitate self-replication and the expression of genes. It would be difficult to argue for the proposition that a simpler structure could attain the same result, or how DNA could rise to its current level of complexity, considering how fundamental its structure is for its function. This is one of the problems that the students of abiogenesis should need to be able to solve. It is easy to figure out why there are four bases, why they are paired, why a codon is three bases in length, why codons code 20 specific amino acids, why the genetic code is degenerate, why DNA is made from two strands, and why coding strands exist, but how they became what they are, is not. That being the case, if you wanted to know how simple molecules made all of this, you would have to start at those simple molecules and not at the much more complex result, which makes the problem of the origin of DNA that much harder to solve. What chemicals involved in what processes could have produced DNA, and how could we ever hope to answer that question? It's like a puzzle box with few or no pieces inside, and you have to figure out how the nonexistent pieces of simple chemicals and processes fit together based on the picture of DNA on the box. You can recreate the pieces as you wish and make the picture whole, but the chance of remaking the exact same pieces that existed in the past is very low, assuming, of course that those puzzle pieces from the past once existed to begin with. If there is no abiogenesis, then there is no puzzle to solve because all the pieces were just made up fantasies.

The simplest organisms known to man all have DNA and reproduce the same way. There are no evidence that single-celled organisms descend from simpler organisms and, if they do, we would need to determine how to make organisms simpler without breaking them completely. This is possible, however, not to the extent where it could help us understand what the previous stage of abiogenesis was, or any stage of abiogenesis, for that matter. The problem with stripping as many genes as we can from DNA is that eventually we reach a point where things cease to function, or the cell becomes completely dependent on the chemicals in its own environment. Even the most stripped-down cells grown in laboratories have nucleic acids, amino acids, and use a genetic code, or some part of it, and fundamentally function the same way as normal cells. The structure of the cell does not seem to contain any hints regarding its true origin, so going at the problem from this direction will result in limited success. Conversely, trying to build living beings from simple molecules has become a popular subject of abiogenesis, owing to the fact that most study done in this area is purely theoretical and speculative.

One popular theory is the RNA World hypothesis, which postulates that RNA and not DNA was the original device to store genetic information. The RNA-first World could solve some issues in theory; however, this idea is yet to be demonstrated in practice. As most molecular machines involved in replication contain lots of RNA, the need to make a different type of molecule, such as DNA, would be eliminated. Some RNA molecules can also self-replicate to a limited extent because they are made of a special sequence of nucleic bases. As long as there's an appropriate number of specific nucleic acids, RNA should be able to replicate itself. Nevertheless, this approach also has its own flaws. RNA is much less stable and durable than DNA, so even keeping it together in one piece becomes an issue. The bigger problem with this theory is the transfer from an RNA-based to a DNA-based system and the simple question of how and why proteins got encoded into RNA. The most crucial sequence of bases in DNA are genes that define proteins, but why would a self-replicating

RNA require any of that? It is capable of multiplying without a need for amino acids, and the order of nucleobases that form its core are responsible for its function as a self-replicating unit and nothing else. Why would such a molecule code for anything protein or DNA-related? What would be the point of acquiring such features? If nucleobases are in abundance in the environment, then why does this organism need to improve itself to a higher level, other than the fact that this is the expectation driven by the theory? And, if it can run out of nucleobases, it needs to self-replicate, isn't it more likely that it will actually run out and stop replicating? If you put bacteria in a Petri dish with food and keep it sealed for a few years what is the most likely outcome? That the bacteria will eat all the food and, after there's no more food, it finds a way to consume the Petri dish and escapes? Or that the bacteria will eventually starve? What is the likelihood of the former compared with simple extinction? If you put the right molecules in the right place at the right time, you can make anything work, but if you put any type of RNA in an uncontrolled environment, the only result will be a molecule that gets broken apart or stops functioning, or both, and at present no research exists that should make us believe otherwise.

Research on abiogenesis only explores chemical problems: how this or that molecule could arise from chemical interactions and what is the least bit of organization that is required to kick start evolution? The problem is that even the simplest cell is quite complex and is only simple compared with much more complex organisms. All cells are information-processing and -preserving units that function using codes, which makes them substantially different compared with the rest of the universe. Information in the form of data is such a leap forward in evolutionary terms that it is hard to even comprehend the minimal requirements for the creation of a system of molecules that could create and process it. Just think about how much time it took for humans to come up with a comprehensive way of writing on clay tablets. With our huge brains, it took us thousands of years, and many civilizations never even got to the point of creating their own writing system. We already had large brains and a spoken language before we chiseled the first letters into a rock. At some point, life had to have changed from a chemical system like self-replicating RNA to a data-driven system, like DNA, nullifying any and all chemical-replicating capacity the precursor of the cell may have had. This may have been a long process; however, the transformation was so thorough that no remnant of the proto cell has survived, not even in the form of bacterial vestiges. Both the cells and their vestiges seem to have disappeared from the face of the Earth, which leads us to the obvious question: were they there to begin with?

There's one even more fundamental problem with the way the cell is set up in relation to the question of abiogenesis. This issue is a simple information paradox, the genetic equivalent of the chicken and the egg problem. Evolution can only bring us as far as the roots of the tree of life go, and eventually we reach a point in time where it stops completely, and at that point, we find problems so fundamentally difficult to solve that most would rather excuse themselves from thinking about them. Let us take the ribosome, the molecular machine that turns messenger RNA into proteins, as our first example. Close to half of the molecular weight of the ribosome is made of proteins, which, in turn, are created by the ribosome itself. You can see how this fact can be considered somewhat problematic. You need proteins to make the ribosome and you need the ribosome to make proteins. There's no factual evidence supporting the idea that a protein-less ribosome would function sufficiently well to be able to produce proteins, or that such a thing has ever existed in the past. For the next example, we can look at all the enzymes that are involved in gene expression, such as RNA polymerase. These enzymes are necessary to express any and all genes stored in DNA; however, they themselves are also stored in DNA as genes. Imagine the case if we had DNA, but no enzymes, then we wouldn't be able to create them because we need the enzymes to read and interpret the base sequence stored in the genes of DNA. Alternatively, if we had the enzymes but no DNA, then there would be nothing to be read and interpreted by the enzymes. For the system to work, the enzymes must exist inside DNA in the form of genes and also outside DNA as physical molecules simultaneously. You need both the genes and the enzymes that express the genes to have a self-sufficient system.

One solution to this problem would be molecular evolution, if it was possible to demonstrate that such a thing could work. Molecular evolution postulates that molecular structures evolved in a similar fashion to living creatures, until such a structure was assembled that was capable of biological evolution. The problem with any such hypothesis is not whether such things are possible because, of course, everything is possible, but whether we have good reasons to believe that they did, in fact, happen. The question is, is it likely to have happened based on our understanding of the universe and its laws or is it not? It is not self-explanatory that it did, despite what many seem to believe, because even though anything is possible in science, nothing, and I mean absolutely nothing, can be considered true without proof. If it could be, science could not exist, as at the very beginning of scientific discoveries nothing, no law and no theory existed. Everything had to be discovered, and while many of the past theories may seem self-explanatory to us today, they really weren't when they were first formulated.

Perhaps, a simple thought exercise could provide better insight into why the issues mentioned previously pose a problem to scientific thought. Let's suppose, for the argument's sake, that we believe that aliens exist. This is not a farfetched idea, as the theory of evolution has effectively removed any barriers to living organisms developing in a way that would bind them to a single planet. In our time, it wouldn't surprise anyone to find life in other solar systems, even though we have never observed alien life outside our home planet. Let us also suppose, that we can travel between the galaxies with ease, and we could land on the surface of any planet we desire to visit. So, what do we do? We believe aliens exist, so we visit all the planets that we believe could sustain life. NASA has already identified many places that meet that requirement already. So, we visit them and let's say that we find nothing. Okay, we still have lots of planets and even solar systems we haven't visited, so let's visit those as well to prove our hypothesis. Suppose we run out of planets to visit yet still find nothing; will our obsessive dedication to our theory dwindle? Likely not; we'll still have lots of asteroids and comets to check, so we'll check them as well. If we again have no luck, we'll decide that we have only checked the surface of all the planets and asteroids and so on. We can check the inside of all of these stellar objects, by drilling down or using some other methods to see if there's life inside of them or not. If we do that and, once again, we find nothing, do you know where we haven't looked yet? The stars! There's lots of room in the stars, plenty for many living beings and advanced civilizations, so we might as well check them as well. From this thought exercise, you can see how our reasonable theory has over time deteriorated into complete nonsense because we couldn't fathom the idea that our original assumption wasn't true. We went from checking the surface of the most likely planets to going inside of stars simply because our assumptions regarding the universe were not validated. At what point should we have stopped and asked ourselves, what if there are no aliens? What if they don't exist? Surely, we should have reexamined our premises sometime before we looked under the last speck of space dust for extraterrestrials that never existed to begin with.

In the same vein, perhaps, we should ask ourselves why we can't come up with a good theory for abiogenesis before we combine every type of molecule produced by every possible chemical reaction known to man. Almost everyone agrees that no good theory exists at the moment, but the real question that must be asked then is why? It is not what we don't know, but rather what we do know that prevents us from moving forward. New theories for the origins of life were quite popular until the importance and function of DNA were discovered. It was only after the science of molecular biology had matured that origin of life studies ground to a halt. It could be that the process that created life was nothing special, that it was nothing more than a sequence of improbable events that are also happening somewhere else in the galaxy, at this very moment; but, is that idea based on what we can see or is it just wishful thinking? Can we see any such process anywhere we are able to look? Certainly, the universe is vast, and it contains many things we cannot see, but is that reason enough to believe that it contains aliens or life-creating chemical reactions we can't even guess what they are really like?

However, why do we care about abiogenesis so much? Evolution starts only after we got the first living organism and not a second before, so what difference does it make how the first living being came to be? It makes a difference because the theory of evolution predicted abiogenesis and because the theory is unique in that it requires it or at least expects it to have happened. Not all theories need it. Biogenesis, for example, had no concept for a beginning, as it had imagined life as an endless circle with no beginning to speak of. Evolution made a beginning necessary and, when that beginning can no longer be explained by any theory, it becomes detrimental to both abiogenesis and evolution. Think about it this way: let's say that life indeed had a beginning, but did not began in the primordial soup, but rather came to be from some external influence that we can't even imagine. If that were the case, couldn't this esoteric force be also responsible for other living beings and not just the first ones? As soon as abiogenesis is removed from the picture, a new contender could arrive to challenge the supremacy of evolution because if one simple organism cannot be explained by causes now in motion, then all organisms are now less likely to be the result of a process like evolution. This makes abiogenesis essential in a philosophical sense, but not necessarily essential in a scientific sense. A scientist could always state that evolution is independent of abiogenesis, but a world in which abiogenesis is plausible and a world where it is not are light years apart, and that detail should not be forgotten. A chain is only as good as its weakest link, and if the chain between living and nonliving matter is broken, the theory of evolution will never be complete.

Chapter 4

Mutating Randomness

To understand the nature of genetic mutations, we need to learn about the fundamentals of molecular biology. I hope the previous chapter helped you gain insight into the role DNA plays in facilitating gene expression and how every aspect of molecular life is controlled by the information stored in DNA. Random genetic mutations are a must-have for evolution to work, as mutations are the only agents that can unpredictably change DNA. Genomic shuffling can only shuffle the genes inside a population or species, but mutations can alter DNA and the genome contained within, without limits, or at least that is what the modern theory of evolution seems to suggest. Even though mutations are unpredictable, the types of mutations likely to happen are limited in both number and scope, and their effects are mostly predictable.

Some mutations are rather esoteric and often harmful, as they involve genetic material gained or injected into the genome without involving the process of reproduction. One such case is when a viral infection adds its own genetic material to the DNA of the host and, consequently, mutates the cell's genome. Not all such injections are inheritable, but many are. While most viral infections are harmful to the host, if the virulent part of the virus is suppressed, the genetic code of the virus may live on in the DNA of the species for as long as the species exists. This way, viruses can add their own genes to the genome of the species they infect. When the virulence of a virus is suppressed, only its remnant remains in the genome, which is commonly referred to as an endogenous retrovirus (ERV). It is believed that ERVs constitute close to one-tenth of the human genome.

Another form of mutation happens when one organism consumes the genetic material of another organism. This is something that only bacteria can do. Many bacteria can consume DNA from the same species, but some can even consume the DNA from a different species of bacteria as well. Usually, they consume and integrate the DNA from the cells close to them that are no longer alive. This way, they can gain genes that were not previously found in the bacteria population, potentially altering the genome of the species forever. Not all bacteria can consume genetic material, and not all can consume the genes of other species, but the ones that do can mutate their own genome this way.

The most common mutations are the ones that happen during the processes of DNA repair or replication. When DNA is damaged by radiation or a chemical agent, the cell tries to fix it by adding back the lost nucleobases to the damaged strand, gluing everything back together. Sometimes, this process puts back the wrong bases instead of the original ones because it can't correctly work out what went missing or because there was an error in the repair process itself; this results in the base sequence changing, in other words, a gene mutation. Mutations happen more often during DNA replication because during replication, the entire genome must be copied, which can result in replication errors and mutations. Different species try to mitigate the risk of mutations by using different mechanisms, but the more complex the species, the more sophisticated this process is, and the less likely it is that mutations will happen as a consequence.

Mutations that occur during the process of replication fall into three categories. Point mutations can change a nucleobase into a different nucleobase, shift mutations add extra bases into the genes, and duplication may cause entire genes to be copied over.

A point mutation is when one base, for example, a thymine is turned into a different nucleobase, such as guanine, which could potentially alter the meaning of the codon the base belongs to. The codon might code for a different amino acid from that point on or affect a genetic regulatory system or process in some way. Most of the genome contains code that regulates gene expressions rather than the genes that code the proteins; therefore, a mutation can easily throw a monkey wrench into the regulatory system even without affecting any gene directly. Many point mutations are neutral, but others might be harmful or even deadly for the cell that is unfortunate enough to have undergone a mutation. Some of them may exert a positive impact on the cell as well, but such cases are very rare. Still, to suggest that point mutations positive or otherwise can't survive would be incorrect, as they are very common; so, there's a very good chance that some of them will endure over subsequent generations.

A shift mutation happens when several nucleobases are added or subtracted from DNA. For example, if an adenine is added to a protein-coding gene with the codons CUU, CUC, CUA, and so on, changing them to ACU, UCU, CCU, A, and so on, the first three amino acids would change from leucine, leucine, leucine to threonine, serine, and proline. The rest of the codons and the amino acids they code would change as well, so the likelihood that such mutations would be positive is very low. Shift mutations can alter large chunks of the genome, but the more they change, the more likely the change will be hazardous to the cell. In addition, a shift mutation might also change the stop codon to something else, essentially making the process of transcription continue rather than stopping at the end of the gene. The same mutation can change a normal codon into a stop codon as well, making transcription end prematurely. There are numerous ways shift mutation can cause harm, and there are many, many diseases associated with this mutation type.

Gene duplication happens when a large chunk of DNA is copied to a new place, usually because of some error during the replication process; this can easily result in one or more duplicated genes. It is broadly believed that gene duplication is an essential part of evolution, as it is one of the few ways the size of the genome can increase. As the new genes are likely to contain the exact same base sequence as the genes they were duplicated from, it is possible that they won't cause much harm to the cell itself. These new genes can be mutated by other types of mutagens, which might result in the acquisition of functions the original genes didn't possess. The genome size of bacteria and animals differs by multiple orders of magnitude, so a mechanism that can produce new genes quickly is crucial for the process of evolution. Proving that a particular gene was originally a duplicate of another gene can be challenging because the genes in question are very different in the present where they can be observed, and past gene duplications can only be presumed from a shared base sequence. It may be true that such genes share a common history; however, it might also be true that their similarities are the result of some other factor(s) rather than being caused by gene duplication. This, of course, wouldn't imply that none of the genes we observe today was originally a duplicate, but it does signify that we have to be more careful when we identify such events as a rule rather than an exception to a rule. Either the rule or the exception to the rule is possible, but the likelihood of one or the other is far from equal.

Mutations are random. They are not the product of any genetic mechanism required or created by the cell itself. They are a byproduct of the cell's mechanism to preserve and protect information stored in DNA. The cell does everything to minimize the effects of mutations and their occurrence, but no such system could possibly be perfect at the scale the cell operates. All life, even the simplest forms, can proofread and fix DNA strands during the process of replication. The cell is aware, in a chemical sense, of the likelihood of mutations occurring and the threat it poses to the integrity of the whole machine; so, it employs many types of error-correcting mechanisms, depending on the complexity of the cell in question. Such needs and behavior are not limited to the biological world. Many modern storage devices have similar problems and solutions as the ones confronting the cell.

For example, the compact disc or CD, a popular transportable storage device from the past, was used to store data in an optical format capable of error correction. CD burners contained lasers to write on discs, but these lasers weren't completely reliable. On a CD, the bits, in other words the "zeroes" and "ones," had to be written close to each other so that the maximum amount of data could be stored, meaning that the laser had to burn holes into the disc that were only a few nanometers apart. The laser would occasionally make errors, which could be detected by the machine during the proofreading process and were fixed by writing to a special zone that could store error-correction bits. The cell's DNA proofreading mechanism works similar to the CD burner's error-correcting process, except that it does not require these special zones because it can just remake the part where the error was found and fix the issue on demand.

The cell has many ways to fix mutations, and the more complex the living being, the more sophisticated and efficient this correction mechanism gets. More complex beings have longer DNA strands, and the likelihood of errors increases with the length of the strand. However, this is probably not the main reason why complex organisms, such as animals and plants, have better error-correcting capabilities compared with bacteria. I believe that single-celled organisms do not possess more sophisticated machinery to detect errors because of the simple fact that mutations do not pose as much a threat to them as a species as mutations do to a complex multicellular organism. If a single bacterium mutates and dies as a result of that mutation, there would still likely be billions of bacteria in the vicinity with the same genes that could take its place, so the species would not be in much danger. That doesn't mean that mutations can't cause harm to lower forms of life, but it does mean that the threat would be contained; so, if the mutation rate is controlled to a degree, the damage to the species would most likely be minimal. If proofreading does not detect a lethal error during division, the energy and material used to create the new bacteria will end up being wasted. While having better error detection might seem desirable, we must also bear in mind that better error detection can also become a waste of resources. In the case of a single-celled organism, the issue would be contained, so the problem could not spread, but a multicellular organism might not be that lucky. A single mutant cell can potentially kill the whole organism if the mutations are that severe. For example, think of cancer; it forces a cell to divide until there is nothing else to consume because it had by that time killed the host. The cells in an animal's body are regulated so that, even if food is abundant, it will normally not divide without limit, but most single-celled organisms are different. They are more than happy to divide whenever possible. Bacteria essentially behave like cancer cells, but without a large organism to harm, this behavior is not that much of an issue. This is the difference between single and multicellular life forms, and this is why I believe that correcting mutations is far more important for our survival than it is for the survival of bacteria.

According to the modern theory of evolution, nature favors beneficial mutations over negative ones, and fitter specimens over less-fit ones, and this is how new species are eventually created. Nature is more likely to select and propagate positive and sometimes neutral mutations and less likely to keep negative ones that are detrimental to the organism. This makes perfect sense. However, we should remember how organisms in general have reacted to the prospect of mutations and what that means for the process of evolution. Organisms both large and small, simple and complex, do everything within their means to minimize the possibility of mutations occurring or affecting the organism itself. Even the genetic code was arranged in a way that minimizes the chance of mutations changing the structure of proteins, and the proofreading of the cell during DNA replication can fix most of the errors that don't fall into that category. All of this is set up so that mutations, both positive and negative, won't affect the cell in any significant way. Life is much more interested in avoiding harmful mutations rather than gaining the advantages from beneficial mutations that are required to advance the process of evolution. Nature clearly believes that living beings are more likely to survive if they have fewer mutations, even if that means less genetic diversity and ultimately less speciation. Natural selection has picked stagnation as the best means of survival over the prospects of evolution. Evolution is the result of mutations that the organism, despite its best efforts, couldn't fix. It is a failure of the system that life devised to keep the species intact over an indefinite number of generations.

Given how much effort the cell takes to fight mutations, it is crucial for the theory of evolution to emphasize that most mutations are harmful and that the cell's defense mechanisms exist only because negative mutations are far more likely to occur than beneficial mutations. It is a commonly accepted fact that, at any given time, more negative mutations can occur in a specific organism than positive, and a failure to defend against all mutations is detrimental to the organism. It might seem self-explanatory that most mutations are not positive, but even if it is, we should ask why it is so. Darwin certainly never believed that the "monstrosities" that were later discovered to be the result of mutations were caused by the same processes that are now believed to have created the new variations necessary for speciation. For Darwin, the changes he observed that created the monstrosities were too detrimental or simply not beneficial for the organism to propagate. They were not very gradual and were also quite rare; so, he believed that the chance of survival of such features was negligible. The monstrosities were the result of negative mutations, and Darwin could not believe that phenomena such as mutations could be responsible for evolution. Who could blame him? The idea of a mutation being positive is just as radical as a statement of fact as a monstrosity being superior to an earlier specimen would be. After all, in what other field is the force responsible for the progress of its subjects describable as pure chance? Extraordinary ideas require extraordinary evidence, and they should not be accepted as fact before the proof is provided, and evolution by natural selection is not exempt from this rule.

Mutations are not unique to nature. They can happen in any system where the same information gets copied over and over and over. For example, historical documents, such as the Bible, had to be copied by scribes many times the past two millennia so that they could be preserved and, consequently, the contents changed somewhat over time. Making copies of books as long as the Bible, using only pen and paper, inadvertently resulted in mistakes by the scribes. Most of these mistakes were small and did not change the meaning of the text much; however, some were much more grievous. According to Prof. Bart D. Ehrman, sometimes scribes accidentally left out entire lines and sometimes entire pages from their manuscripts, creating variations of the gospels that never existed before. Caspar René Gregory mentions that there exists a copy of the new testament written a thousand years ago where the genealogy of Jesus got messed up so much that someone named Phares became the first man to exist instead of Adam, and he also became the creator of the world, taking God's place who was written off as the son of Aram. Such literary monstrosities do exist, but because these copies were quite bad, they were rarely copied over. You could say that the selective pressure against them was quite high. In contrast, the unintentional mistakes that would propagate were the ones that didn't change the meaning of the text and that is why they were not noticed until researchers started comparing them to earlier texts. We could think of these changes as the neutral mutations of the holy scripture. There are numerous changes that fall into this category, tens of thousands, in fact, but just as when they happen to living organisms, these mutations don't change the meaning and function of the organism or book in question regardless of their quantity.

The Bible has been the victim of both neutral and negative mutations, but surely nothing could improve the original text, right? No change could be seen as a beneficial mutation, right? From a purely evolutionary viewpoint, that is definitely not the case, as some changes were kept precisely because the scribes believed that they improved the text. The most well-known of these changes was the addition of a story regarding a woman who committed adultery and Jesus who saved her by stating: *"He that is without sin among you, let him cast the first stone at her."* This tale was added to the Gospel of John around the same time the horrific genealogy of Jesus was written down, roughly a thousand years after the original gospel was created. The only difference between these two biblical alterations is that one was kept, and the other was forgotten. The people who read and copied the text selected the story as something that improved the text, and that is why it survived and is so well-known today. Only a few such changes have been identified in biblical history, but one thing that makes these special is that none of them was an accident. These changes could be recognized as beneficial mutations, but not the same kind as we expect to find in nature. These mutations were not random, and they were not guided by a process that was independent of the method of selection. Even if we believe that the stories were not kept intentionally, their addition was certainly not accidental.

From the example of the Bible, we can see that truly random beneficial mutations in the New Testament or in the earlier writings that preceded it are quite rare or simply nonexistent. It is true that the originals were altered thousands of times by accident, but these changes never enhanced the texts in any meaningful way. If evolution as a general concept can work on any type of material that has been copied over a long span of time, then we should ask why it hasn't improved any of the gospels, by adding new stories to it or by altering old ones? We know that such changes have been done for better or worse by conscious agents, so the possibility is clearly there for evolution to work its magic, and yet it doesn't. Maybe there wasn't sufficient time for evolution to take full advantage of the mistakes of the scribes, and that is, indeed, a possibility, but most definitely not the only one, and we must be careful to not turn this possibility into an excuse. At the end of the day, the process of evolution did not improve the Bible the way it had improved organisms in the past. The evidence is consistent with the possibility of the Bible becoming far better in the next few million years owing to evolution and also with the Bible not improving at all over the same span of time owing to stagnation. However, one thing is clear, the existence and effects of beneficial mutations are not self-evident.

Just imagine what would it take to improve your favorite book by evolutionary means. If we added or changed random words or repeated whole sentences after one another, how long would it take for you to recognize a new copy as superior? Alternatively, if we shifted the letters and changed each letter to the next position on the alphabet in every word inside a paragraph, the way shift mutations changes genes, how long would it take before we could get an intelligible sentence via that method, let alone something that improves the quality of a book? The idea that, given sufficient time, any book can be changed into a different book with a new and improved story is convenient, as no one can confirm or deny such claims. Even changing a single sentence for the better, without the help of an intelligent agent, takes enormous effort, if such a thing is even possible to begin with. Most words cannot be replaced with most other words, and adding new words between words is just as hard. Changing letters or adding letters to a word has the same issue. Sure, if you try long enough, you may improve a sentence or even the book the sentence belongs to, but can you turn a romance novel into a detective book this way? That is something evolution can do. It turns fish into birds over a very long period of time. The only difference is that written language is far more malleable than the language of the cell, and the information contained in DNA is much more interlinked and, therefore, can take a lot less abuse before it breaks down compared with any written book. The story in a book can survive some harm, but the cell is different, and the same number of changes to a cell can make it unsustainable, while in the case of a book, it would only cause a minor inconvenience to the reader. The main reason that the harmful effects of mutations are often mitigated is that when they happen in a cell, there are thousands of other cells in its proximity that can replace that cell. The only truly dangerous mutations, except for the ones that cause cancer, are the ones that get inherited because they could affect all the cells in a population negatively. These mutations are often invisible to us because they are naturally selected out, but they are also the ones that evolution requires for its own progress.

The universe can be a strange place to live in, so what may or may not make sense to a human being is generally not a good measure of truth. The strange indeterministic world of quantum mechanics has baffled scientists and common folk equally for some time. The very idea of superposition, where a particle is not in any state and will only gain one when it is observed or rather interacts with something, is fundamentally different from what we humans can experience in our macroscopic world. Many have objected to the idea of superposition and claimed that just because the state of a particle hasn't been measured doesn't mean it is stateless, but as far as science is considered, the existence of superposition has been proven beyond any reasonable doubt. That is how strange our universe really is, and that is why our hopes and beliefs regarding its true nature are completely inconsequential. However, we often forget how much our personal experience can cloud our judgment, and that is why we need the scientific method to separate the few good ideas we have from the unquantifiable many that we believe in. At the end of the day, evidence is all that matters; so, even if beneficial mutations creating new species is a radical proposition, it doesn't matter as long as we have the evidence to back up that proposition.

According to the theory of evolution, all forms of life, all variations, and all species have acquired their current state of diversification by experiencing and going through numerous beneficial mutations over thousands of millennia. You might expect that to discover evidence for a phenomenon literally responsible for everything that is alive today would be quite easy to find in nature, but the reality is that, at the moment, beneficial mutations are the rarest commodity on planet Earth. Of course, this might change in the future, but right now, it is unlikely that a person would need more than one hand to count every instance known to man. That is how rare confirmed cases are. This could be because it is challenging to discover and validate beneficial mutations, even though people have been searching for them for decades, but it is also possible that they are simply extremely rare. The latter possibility is not considered mainstream in the scientific community. Still, we have to work with what we have and, perhaps, these rare examples of beneficial mutations have what it takes to establish a baseline of thought for the theory of evolution, or at least for further investigation. Meanwhile, we shouldn't allow the fact that some mutations exist to cloud our judgment and accept them as evidence unless they meet a general criterion. In this case, the criteria will be the same as would be for any true cause or *vera causa* of this nature: namely, it must demonstrate the direction and extent evolution has to achieve for it to create the things it is supposedly responsible for, such as organs and molecular machinery. I will refer to this as "potentiality," as in does the mutation have the potential to attain the kind of things it is being used as evidence for?

One of the oldest-known observed changes in the animal kingdom believed to be the result of beneficial mutations is the melanism or darkening of the peppered moth that was observed during the early industrial age. In the nineteenth century, the pollution of coal-burning factories turned the trunks of most trees in certain areas of Great Britain black, causing the light-colored peppered moth, which rested on the trunks, to become an easy target for predators since they stood out much more than they did before. Simultaneously, a new variety of moth, a darker version of the same species, appeared that blended in with the darker trees and, thus, managed to gain prominence. It has not been proven beyond doubt that this darkening of the peppered moth was caused by a muta-tion rather than it being a rare genetic variant that existed before, but the idea is not implausible. We know for a fact that albinism in mammals can be caused by the mutation of a single gene called the TYR gene. If this gene is damaged, then the body can't produce melanin and, consequently, the skin becomes completely white. Albinism is not unique to mammals, so if the color of the peppered moth depends on a similar chemical system, then it is not a stretch to believe that if the amount of a specific chemical increases because of a mutation, then that could possibly turn the moth's entire body much darker. It is a good guess, good enough to use as an example of a beneficial mutation, and almost all evolutionary biologists do. The only question that remains is whether turning a moth or any other species darker or lighter has the potential to create new features akin to the organs' evolution has created over time. Use your imagination. We don't have to observe the appearance of new, novel parts. In this case, it would be adequate to simply imagine it. Just think, what kind of new variation can evolution create from a dark moth that it couldn't create from a lighter one? It's like asking what kind of new story or sentence can be added to a Bible with a dark cover as opposed to one with a white cover. Changing the general color of any animal is simple because the actual color is a minuscule part of the animal's whole genome and because the change is less likely to be detrimental compared with changing, for example, the genes responsible for the animal's internal organs. A black moth is as much of a new species as a human albino would be, and albinos definitely aren't anything remotely close to a new species. The potentiality of melanism for creating new variations or a new species is lacking even inside our almost limitless imagination, not to mention outside of it. The fact that melanism exists proves nothing, or at the very least, not the grand evolutionary processes it is supposed to be an example of.

While it is not certain that mutations caused the darker color of the peppered moth, there are actual cases where we know for sure that the positive attribute was the result of a specific mutation. One such case is related to the disease known as malaria, which is spread by insects mostly in tropical climates and kills about half a million individuals a year. The disease is caused by a microorganism, and it spreads inside the body by latching itself to the red blood cells found in our blood. Using this method, it can move from one place in the body to another, simply by hitchhiking in cells whose job is to transport things such as oxygen to different places in the body. For example, at the end of its life cycle, the parasite can travel to the veins located under the skin where it could be picked up by a hungry mosquito, which could then infect another victim with the parasite. The organism's ability to infect and attach itself to red blood cells is essential for its own survival and, without it, the parasite could not spread as easily to other hosts. A mutation exists in some humans that can cause the red blood cells to change shape, making it hard for the parasite to use them as a convenient traveling vehicle. If a human has this mutation on one of his own chromosomes, but not on both, then the person will acquire something called the sickle-cell trait. When a parasite attaches itself to a red blood cell, the cell takes a sickle-like shape, causing the removal and destruction of the red blood cell; this causes the person to be resistant to the malaria parasite, which is highly advantageous in a place where malaria and mosquitoes are a common occurrence. The people of Africa, who have been living with the parasites for countless eons, are the most likely to encounter malaria, so it is no surprise that the mutation that causes the sickle-cell trait is mostly found in the DNA of native Africans.

The sickle-cell trait and the mutation responsible for it are often-cited examples of evolution by natural selection; however, their evidentiary value in demonstrating the complex transitions of the past might be somewhat overinflated. The trait is caused by a single mutation that causes the adenine of the GAG codon in a single gene to change into thymine, changing the codon to GTG and the amino acid from glutamic acid to valine. This implies that the trait can be inherited purely by chance from someone who doesn't possess it because the mutation only needs to change a single nucleobase in a parent's DNA. Few would argue that a single-point mutation that could improve the survival rate of a population would not be selected by natural selection, but to use this as proof for the creation of new genes that are hundreds or thousands of bases long might be a bit of a stretch. What if a single mutation is not sufficient to advance a species? What if you need a hundred specific mutations to get to the next stage and you can't get there or anywhere else for that matter by simply advancing by one mutation at a time? Why is that possibility excluded from what we are willing to consider?

Everything has limits, and not everything that glitters is gold. Even beneficial mutations selected by nature can have unintended consequences. In the case of the sickle-cell trait, the mutation itself rarely harms the individual; however, if both chromosomes of a person carry the same mutation, it can eventually lead to an illness called sickle cell disease. This disease can cause all types of problems in a person's vascular system and can easily lead to premature death. Hence, while the mutation does help many people survive in some areas of the world, if everyone or most people would carry it, its effects would be worse than malaria. The mutation is only positive as long as someone is more likely to die from malaria than from sickle cell disease. If anything, this mutation demonstrates how difficult it is to change any gene in a species. After all, even though malaria and mosquitoes have been living alongside humans for thousands of years or longer, humans could not acquire any immunity that would not hurt their existence in the long run. In places where malaria is not a threat, the frequency of the mutation in a population decreases naturally, so at best, this mutation is a temporary one. However, not many species possess temporary organs or anything of the sort, so why anyone would champion this mutation as an example of evolution is a bit curious. What is the potential of such mutation to improve the human condition other than by the prospect of completely disappearing from our collective genomes?

If evolution by natural selection finding beneficial mutations has been an everyday occurrence since the day the first
living organism came to be, it is puzzling why evolutionary
biologists could not come up with better examples for mutations, unless there isn't a lot to choose from.

The third example of beneficial mutation covers a set of
commonly occurring mutations associated with the introduction and use of antibiotics. Antibiotics are used to treat bacterial infections and are irreplaceable among the vital medicines
used to treat patients today. These chemical compounds
either kill or inhibit the spread of bacteria; however, owing to
the extensive and improper use of this class of drugs, some
bacteria have become immune to some or most of the antibiotics. Antibacterial resistance is a serious issue in medicine,
and it affects almost everyone living today and not just
humans but other organisms, such as farm animals as well. It
is quite right to suggest that this resistance was acquired by
evolutionary means and that this is, indeed, a modern example
of evolution by natural selection. Nevertheless, it is crucial to
look at antibiotics a bit closer before we jump to further
conclusions regarding the extent of evolution's creative power
related to this phenomenon.

The first major antibiotic was penicillin, which was first
synthesized in 1942, and it soon became a super-cure that
could stop most bacterial infections at the time. Unfortunately, the high and exclusive use of penicillin led to the
creation of new resistant bacteria variants, which highly
diminished the utility of penicillin, thereby creating the need
to discover new wonder drugs that could fight the resistant
bacteria; however, many of these new drugs also became ineffective over time for the same reason penicillin did. Accordingly, by the twentieth century, an obscene number of
antibiotics have been developed, which often differed from

each other by the mode of use and the bacteria they were effective against. Today, some superbugs are resistant to all antibiotics and account for a very high mortality rate, but as long as someone is not infected with one of those, there's a good chance that the person can be cured relatively quickly using antibiotics.

Depending on the type of antibiotic, the drug may inhibit amino acid, nucleic acid, or cell wall synthesis, disrupt the cell membrane, or inhibit the metabolic pathway of bacteria. For example, penicillin and its derivatives are called beta-lactam antibiotics that inhibit cell wall synthesis by binding to the enzymes that construct the cell wall and, by doing so, stop the creation of new bacteria. The original penicillin was found in mold known to have strong antibiotic attributes. Hence, penicillin is a naturally occurring drug, and penicillin-resistant bacteria have existed alongside it for a very long time, but because this drug resistance was useful only to bacteria that lived in the proximity of certain mold fungi, naturally the bacteria that infected animals and humans did not develop such resistance. All of this changed when penicillin became the go-to drug for every illness imaginable, even for those not caused by bacteria. This created a selective pressure where any bacteria resistant to penicillin had a much better chance of survival and could outcompete common variants of the same bacteria that weren't resistant. Eventually, this led to the dominance of the resistant variants, possibly replacing most common strains of the same bacteria species completely. Nevertheless, as long as none of the variants had any resistance to begin with, this scenario could not happen because all variants would be equally at risk from antibiotics. Originally, when penicillin was introduced, this might have been the case, as most bugs that infected humans had most likely not met the antibiotic extensively before the 1940s. Despite such a scenario being likely, in the next 30 years, penicillin lost most of its potency, to the point that now it can only cure a fraction of the infections it originally could.

Bacteria is a very strange life form. It can do things that most other organisms can't. One of those things is that it can consume the DNA remains of dead bacteria in its vicinity and incorporate the contents of the DNA into its own genome. Depending on the bacteria, this can happen within the same species or cross-species; so, even the bacteria that live on or near fungi can trade genes with bacteria that grow on something else completely, such as, in the belly of animals that eat the fungi itself. Viruses can also help in attaining the same result, by taking genes from one bacterium and passing them onto another. With these methods, resistant bacteria can easily pass their genes to other types of nonresistant bacteria, making them resistant as well. In the case of penicillin, the drug used something called a beta-lactam ring that could bond to enzymes necessary for the construction of the cell wall, but resistant bacteria had an enzyme called beta-lactamase that could break the beta-lactam ring of penicillin, rendering it useless. Over time, the gene responsible for the beta-lactamase enzyme had been passed on from one bacterium to many others and, eventually, most variants of infectious bacteria became resistant to penicillin. Such genetic changes can be viewed as examples of evolutionary development; however; the very factor that makes such variations conceivable is the fact that bacteria can cannibalize the DNA of other bacteria and gain genetic material via this process. This makes the whole notion of species in the microbiological world a lot more complicated, as one bacterium can easily take genes from another becoming more like that bacteria and less like its own ancestors. The new bacteria become a de jure descendant of both bacteria species, which is not that different from the traditional chromosomal shuffling of genes that happens during the reproduction phase of higher forms of life. In this respect, the process is not really evolutionary in the strictest sense, or at least not more than gaining a mixture of genes via simple biological reproduction would be. No new genes and no new enzymes are created by this process. Although bacteria reproduce asexually, they can draw from a much larger gene pool compared with any sexually reproducing organism, which implies that as long as the gene pool contains the necessary genes, they can adapt to environmental changes much faster than any complex organism can. If the genes that cause antibiotic resistance don't exist anywhere in this large gene pool, then no bacteria can assimilate them, and none will be able to produce the enzymes that are responsible for the resistance.

Adapting the enzymes of the greater bacterial gene pool is not the only way bacteria can develop resistance to antibiotics. For example, when penicillin is used to treat an infection, it does so by chemically binding to the cell wall's molecules during cell division. That is, penicillin has a specific molecular shape that can bind to a specific molecular structure, effectively disabling whatever it is binding to. However, if the structure changes just a little bit, then penicillin might have difficulty binding to it, rendering the bacteria and its offspring resistant to the antibiotic. Most point mutations that affect the cell wall are normally detrimental or deadly to the organism; however, there are some that can change it just enough to not cause irrevocable damage while, at the same time, give the bacteria resistance to antibiotics like penicillin. Given the high reproductive rate of bacteria and the extreme environmental pressure antibiotics are putting them under, it is no surprise that, if slight adjustments to a specific gene or genes in the DNA can help the bacteria survive, then natural selection would eventually find those genes and alter them accordingly. With every new bacterium created, there's a chance that a new resistant strain is born and, as a bacteria's division only takes a few minutes, there's a good chance that nature will find one sooner or later. When such things happen, medical scientists need to create or discover new antibiotics that harmful bacteria aren't resistant against, until they do become resistant, thereby repeating the cycle until one of us can no longer adapt.

The rapid growth of antibacterial resistance might seem to suggest that evolution can create new strains of bacteria without much effort, nevertheless we must not forget what antibiotics are and where they came from. Penicillin is a molecule created by mold that competes with bacteria and uses penicillin to kill as much bacteria as possible so that it can consume more nourishment than it otherwise could. The mold kills bacteria around itself rather than internally, which is why biologists discovered its antibacterial properties because many cultures have used it to fight infections for eons, to protect certain items from decay. Penicillin was never meant for human consumption, or any type of consumption for that matter. It was merely a stroke of luck and some ingenuity and a lot of hard work that allowed penicillin to become a miracle drug, even if only temporarily. Originally, it was a simple drug used by a simple organism for a simple purpose, and it had fulfilled that purpose for millions of years; however, for the treatment of complex animals, such as humans, it was simply not that great, or at least not for long. Antibiotics may be the best way to treat patients to cure bacterial infections, but it is far from being the deadliest threat any bacteria that finds itself inside the belly of an animal must face. Humans can and do fight infections even without the aid of antibiotics. The immune system has its own cells tasked with destroying any unwanted invader and, only in the rare case when that fails, do we require the aid of antibiotics.

The body has two types of immune systems or rather has two distinct parts of the same system that function differently. The first type is the innate immune system, which tries to eliminate pathogens as soon as they enter the body and, therefore, uses a generic approach to destroy as many invaders as possible before they could spread anywhere else. This system functions in a similar manner to antibiotics in that both agents use a wide vector to attack pathogens and are effective against most infections, though they are also doomed to be ineffective against super-resistant bacteria. The only difference is that the innate immune system tends to spare beneficial bacteria, while most antibiotics kill indiscriminately, which is why they tend to upset the stomach and cause other side effects. Taking antibiotics is like carpet bombing the digestive system and, while the innate immune system attempts to constrain the destruction to the location of the enemy, antibiotics tend to burn both friend and foe. Both methods were made to handle opposition, but neither is without their own drawback. One focuses on the opponent's armament inside only a specific territory, while the other tries to level the whole district. If the opponent can hide itself, then both methods become ineffective, and that is how resistant bacteria can beat both the innate immune system and antibiotics.

The more advanced second part of the body's defense system is the adaptive immune system, which goes into action if the innate system cannot cope with the intruders effectively. The adaptive system uses lymphocyte cells to find and destroy invaders but, rather than using general rules to recognize pathogens, it can differentiate between the host's cells and any potential invader. These lymphocyte cells can bind to small protein structures located on the surface of other cells and use them to identify the cells and recognize them as either friend or foe. These surface protein structures, unique to every cell variant and bacteria strand, are called epitopes. Each lymphocyte is created with the ability to bind to several randomly arranged epitope variants, and together they can bind to every cell imaginable. Of course, only some lymphocytes can bind to specific invaders, or in this case antigens, with specific epitopes, but there are so many lymphocyte variants in the body, some of them are bound to match. Unfortunately, this also means that there are some lymphocytes that can match with the body's own cells as well, as those too have their unique epitopes on their own surface. To avoid the immune system killing the host's cells, the first time lymphocytes are created, they roam around the body trying to bind to any cell they can find. Any lymphocyte that manages to bind to one of the host's cells or friendly bacteria living inside the host is mercilessly destroyed, ensuring that only lymphocytes that don't recognize the host and its allies are retained. The remaining lymphocytes recognize foreign antigens and, when they do, they get activated and immediately start self-replicating until they gather a force large enough to destroy the antigens. This way, the adaptive immune system can recognize any potential invader rather than relying on predetermined chemical factors that may or may not help in the removal of the invading pathogens. It is like a bunker buster bomb that can penetrate several meters of concrete. It can destroy almost anything, but you need to know where to drop it; else, it's useless. The adaptive system also memorizes the epitopes of the vanquished foe; so, the next time the immune system has to manage the invasion, there will be several lymphocytes in the body that can take action, making the body virtually immune as long as it remembers the pathogens.

The adaptive immune system is the type of enemy that

bacteria has a difficult time dealing with, as no matter how many times the bacteria alter their own structures, the adaptive system is most likely able to adapt to it. Unfortunately, it takes time for the adaptive system to start working after a person gets infected with the invader and, depending on the infection, the individual may die during the first two or three days when the system is still passive. Nevertheless, the body's own immune system is still more reliable against bacteria in the long run compared with most antibiotics. This is why the HIV virus, which attacks the lymphocytes and disables the adaptive immune system, used to be a guaranteed death sentence. The virus itself can't kill the body, but the many pathogens it allows to enter eventually overcome whatever antibiotics or vitality the body still had. Even so, antibiotics were and still are the best medicine to fight bacteria after the immune system; however, that doesn't make them a great way to fight infections in general, especially if you consider what kind of medicines might be developed in the near future.

All of our technology eventually becomes obsolete. For example, computers are amazing. They are amazing today, they were amazing 10 years ago, and they were amazing 20 and 30 years ago as well. All these statements are true, and yet any computer older than 10 years is considered complete and utter garbage by today's standards. That is how we will look at antibiotics eventually in the future, as nothing more than the simple medicines of a more primitive era. The reason bacteria can evolve resistance against antibiotics is not that bacteria are so good at evolving new ways of attacking victims, but because antibiotic medicine is a simple nonadaptive solution that even bacterial evolution can overcome. Indeed, bacteria may evolve thousands of times faster than primates do, but when you are traveling at the speed of a snail, even the speed of an ant could be considered superfast. The changes bacteria go through have little consequence for our predictions related to evolution, if all it does is to slightly alter the existing structures or move structures from one organism to another. Depending on your interpretation of the evidence, you might see bacteria being able to resist modern drugs as an example of evolution's great ability to change or the narrow limits within which it can change. Such evidence should be considered insufficient and unsatisfactory from any reasonable standpoint. Any theory that relies on the eye of the beholder to substantiate its claims cannot be viewed as scientific or, at the very least, not to a high degree. To begin with, we need science to avoid such dilemmas and, if we are creating a dilemma rather than avoiding it, then we are not doing it correctly.

In this chapter, I gave an overview of the genetic mutations found in nature where evolution is supposed to have taken place. Unfortunately, examples of beneficial mutations are very hard to find, although not because people have not been looking for them. Even if evolution requires tens of thousands of years to create a new species, if we accept that it does so via gradual change, then beneficial mutations should be observable in a shorter time span as well. There's a lot of uncertainty in this field of study. Are mutations hard to come by because they are very rare or because we are bad at observing them in nature? Perhaps, we require a different approach if we wish to find answers to these questions.

Chapter 5

Testing the Impossible

A s a general rule, when we want to test a theory like evolution, we should always seek the evidence in nature and not in a laboratory. As natural selection acts based on the environmental pressures associated with nature itself, doing tests in a controlled environment can easily produce results that are not very realistic. However, as testing in nature seems to be impossible, we should do the next best thing and understand what kind of insights evolution in a test tube could provide us. We need to recognize that testing in this context doesn't imply that we are testing a falsifiable hypothesis, as that would require a law or a statement that can, in theory, be disproven. Falsifiability is the degree of difficulty necessary to disprove a theory, so if we fail to falsify the theory, we may have a high degree of certainty that it is correct. A failure to falsify a theory does not mean that the theory has high falsifiability, as theories that are vague and don't make many predictions are also hard to falsify. The theory of evolution does not take into account such considerations, so when experiments are conducted, there are no predefined expectations that, if not met, could refute the theory itself. Experiments are conducted to see *how* evolution works and not to determine *if* it works. If, by some miracle, a discrepancy between the theory and the result of experiments is found, the theory is corrected to fit the facts, or the irregularity gets ignored completely. Such interventions are rarely necessary though, because generally, there are no expectations that must be met, to begin with. This does not mean that testing can't be valuable, far from it, but we should not expect to find an earthshaking revelation in the corner of a laboratory if we aren't prepared to make predictions for the theory in advance. That said, the results of these experiments may prove unexpectedly invaluable for future discussions, as the data they provide could potentially be used to confirm or deny the theory of evolution when and if it becomes falsifiable.

The most famous and ground-breaking evolution experiment was conducted by Richard Lenski and his team, beginning in 1988. In this experiment, nearly identical *Escherichia coli* (*E. coli*) bacteria were put into 12 flasks. Each flask contained certain substances, mostly chemicals, that could function as food for *E. coli*. The bacteria consumed the food and reproduced inside the flask but, after 8 hours, the food ran out, and the bacteria started starving, causing it to go into stasis. By the next day, the container was occupied by organisms that were most numerous when the vial ran out of food. At that time, the researchers took a sample and froze a part of it, while the rest was put into a new flask containing the same type of chemicals as the previous flask. This process was repeated each day for at least three decades, which is why this experiment was aptly named the long-term evolution experiment (LTEE). The bacteria reached their 50,000th generation in 2010 and, by 2017, the 12 strands had been transferred 10,000 times each, meaning that the experiment had been going for at least 10,000 days straight. As a small portion of bacteria was frozen every day, each sample could be unfrozen at a later date for testing purposes so that certain factors, such as the change in cell size, could be determined for any strand of any generation of the experiment.

Tests were done at several major milestones, such as after reaching 10,000, 20,000, and 50,000 generations. In these tests, bacteria from older generations were unfrozen to determine their size, molecular density, and fitness. By doing so, the attributes of major generations could then be compared, which revealed their trajectories over time. In general, all three observed attributes had increased in all populations and, even though the attributes did not increase at the same rate, their trajectories were always similar to one another. We can state beyond any reasonable doubt that these *E. coli* bacteria had been evolving during the experiment and that the mutations the bacteria acquired were accountable for the increase in several of its major attributes. This is a fact. However, whether these findings support the greater theory of evolution must be determined by careful analysis of the data.

The ability of a laboratory to detect physical factors, such as cell size and cell density, might not surprise anyone, but you might wonder how Richard Lenski and his team measured the fitness of bacteria from different generations. You might recall that Fischer's fundamental theorem of natural selection was based on the concept of fitness and its change over time and, while fitness alone can't verify evolution, it is no doubt connected to the ultimate proof in some way. Either way, fitness is a major factor in determining evolution's validity, so we must understand how Lenski determined its value in relation to the different generations of bacteria. What the team did was very clever. They added a genetic marker to the 12 strands that the original bacteria didn't have. By doing so, they could distinguish any bacteria from a later generation from the bacteria of the original strand, even if they were put into the same environment. When a sample from a newer generation was unfrozen for testing, some of the original strands was also unfrozen, and both specimens were put into the same vial, forcing the old bacteria to compete with the new for the same resources, in the environment the new bacterium was already familiar with. After letting the bacteria grow for a day, the team checked how much of each bacterium from the new and the old strands had remained in the vial. By comparing the two, the fitness of the new generation relative to the old was determined. This is why the ability to tell them apart was crucial in determining their fitness, as otherwise, one could not distinguish a bacterium of one generation from the original *E. coli* and would not be able to determine their distribution ratio when mixed. Relative fitness is called "relative" because every new generation was compared at certain intervals to the exact same bacteria strand that the experiment started with. Consequently, the expected fitness values would be a figure like 150% or 200% if fitness increased by 50% or 100% during the experiment. Relative fitness of 200% implied that, after one day of testing, twice as many *E. coli* from the new, more-evolved strand than the original strand remained in the vial. Thus, it is fair to say that the Lenski team, indeed, determined the fitness of each generation of the bacteria in a meaningful way and that this change was caused by mutations. Their results were both conclusive and, in theory, reproducible, and it appears that more research papers have been written on this subject than on any other topic related to the LTEE, so its importance for the scientific community is undeniable.

The relative fitness of each bacteria strand did, in fact, increase over time, which aligns with the general predictions of the theory of evolution; however, the whole story is slightly more complicated than that. While the increase in fitness was constantly present over any observed time frame, the amount of increase was far from constant and instead was consistently decreasing over time. For example, if we take a look at the average of all 12 strands from generation 0, measuring the change in fitness once at the end of every 10,000 generations, we would get the following result: in the first 10,000 generations, fitness increased by 33%; in the second by 17%; in the third by 6.7%; in the fourth by 9.4%; and in the fifth by only 1%. While the decline of the change in fitness was not constant, the single exception at the 40,000th generation was well within the declared margin of error, and the number did rebound by the 50,000th generation; therefore, it did not affect the expected trajectory significantly. By 2010, the increase in fitness had shrunk to 1% from a whopping 33%, which is quite a lot if we take into account that the 22-year duration of the experiment could not be considered a long time frame by evolutionary standards. *E. coli* has existed for millions of years, so it would be strange to suggest that it gained the last inch of fitness measurable in these past few decades by pure coincidence. Something other than natural selection had to be the cause of the quick increase in fitness and its equally rapid decline in its velocity because if nature could cause *E. coli* to advance as much as it did during the experiment, then it would have already done it a million times over.

If you remove bacteria from its natural habitat and place it into an artificial one inside a test lab, and if the new environment does not precisely mimic the regular habitat that the bacteria was accustomed to, then the new environment will put strong selective pressure on the bacteria, which will most likely lead to some sort of change in its genome. *E. coli* bacteria usually lives inside the intestines of warm-blooded animals, which can be quite diverse; however, such environments still vastly differ from the artificially created conditions of the LTEE. Remember that the bacteria were starved every day on a regular basis for thousands of days, which is slightly different from the difficulties it normally has to endure. Certainly, bacteria such as *E. coli* go through periods with limited or no food present in the environment, but not as often and not as regularly as it did during the experiment. It should come as no surprise that such conditions would enhance the bacteria's ability to survive for longer intervals in environments with low amounts of food present. Growing larger and containing more resources would likely help during extended periods of limited food availability, which explains why both the bacteria's cell size and cell density increased over time during the experiment. The organism that can prevent itself from going into stasis the longest will be the one that can replicate the most. This would naturally increase the relative fitness of the *E. coli* bacteria strand, as long as it stayed in the artificially created environment. However, if it had to compete with the original strand in the original's regular habitat, it is doubtful that it would perform as well as the first-generation bacteria would. After all, relative fitness only measures the bacteria's fitness in the altered environment and not in its natural habitat; therefore, fitness isn't simply relative to the first generation of bacteria, but relative to the new environment as well. These simple observations related to the experiment are, I would argue, self-explanatory, uncontroversial, and generally accepted in the community. There's not that much debate regarding these claims; however, from this point onward, the points I will be making will progressively diverge from the mainstream view.

Several tests were conducted to make it possible to create a model from the fitness data so that a mathematical function could be obtained that would produce the desired fitness values for every past generation and to predict future values. To achieve this, Lenski's team measured the relative fitness of specific bacteria generations that were a specific number of generations apart from each other. This interval was selected because measuring every single generation rather than once per each thousandth generation would have taken too much time. Sometimes measurements were taken hundreds of generations apart but, depending on the test, the distance between two measurements might have been a lot more than that. The distance usually depended on the test in question. Those tests that had smaller scopes, such as 2000 generations, would usually use shorter intervals like a hundred generations, but longer tests that went as far as 10,000 generations used a 500-long interval instead. Subsequent tests would use even longer intervals. That is, shorter tests would produce more fine-grained results, while longer tests could be more accurate in predicting trends simply because they had far more data points, even if those were further apart compared with the points used in the shorter tests. Consequently, the short 2000-generation-long test, which was published in 1991, produced a dataset that could be best fitted with a model that used a step function. When drawn in a two-dimensional coordinate system, step models look similar to stairs viewed from the side. The step shape of the fitness curve fits the data even better if we are only using the data of a single strand rather than all 12 of them.

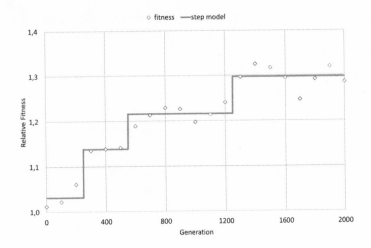

E. Coli ARA-1 Population Fitness

The shape supported the idea that the increase in fitness was because of the effects of mutations as, whenever a beneficial mutation occurred, fitness sharply soared vertically while, between mutations, it stayed flat. This resulted in the shape of the progressively ascending steps, which would have been invisible if the test involved too many strands or the test's interval was too long, as the mutation interval had to be short enough to produce the flat surface of each individual step. The flat parts of the model suggest that it took some time before each significant beneficial mutation was found and, until such an event occurred, fitness was stagnating. This can be explained by the fact that most mutations aren't beneficial and, as a result of the low probability of beneficial mutations, several attempts had to be made before any one of them could be found. In 2004, at the 20,000th generation mark, Lenski estimated that, from the one billion mutations that had occurred by that time, no more than a hundred were fixed for each strand. As this short test only looked at the first 2000 generations, the decline in fitness gains was not very pronounced, but it could still be noticed if you looked at the model carefully.

One of the interesting genetic adaptations that happened past the 2000th generation was the evolution of hyper mutability in 6 of the 12 strands between generations 2500 and 8500. The efficiency and accuracy of DNA repair had markedly diminished in these 6 strands and, therefore, the rate of point mutations increased a hundredfold. The consequence of this event was that the fitness values of the hypermutators overshot the other six's fitness values, creating vertical distance between the trend lines of the two groups in favor of the hypermutators. This distance increased at early generations but did not increase further after the initial boom; so, the hypermutators would grab onto the early fitness gains and not lose them over time. Given how advantageous hypermutability seems, it is strange that none of the other six bacteria strands acquired this trait for the next 40,000 generations. The first six acquired it in only 9000 generations, so this irregularity cannot be a coincidence. The most likely explanation is that hypermutability only helps in the gathering of simple point mutations early on and—as those mutations would be acquired eventually anyway—once that happens, the trait becomes redundant. Hypermutability gives bacteria a head start in an artificial environment but at a cost that more self-restrained bacteria aren't willing to pay. As fitness gains are directly tied to beneficial mutations, preventing the bacteria from fixing them yields gains very quickly, but you can only do that once, and you can only do it at the start, and it might backfire on you on the long run. It is a shortcut on the road to success, one that is thorny and might lead to a future deficit. In the grand scheme of things, a shortcut at best can only hasten the inevitable and do nothing more.

Results of the first large-scale test reaching 10,000 generations were published in 1994, and the findings included a new model for the combined mean fitness data. This new model described a hyperbolic function that clearly illustrated the diminishing nature of the fitness data. Plotting this function in a two-dimensional coordinate system revealed that the curvature of the early fitness gains flattened out over time. This trend continued past the 10,000th generation until a point where the line looked completely flat to the naked eye. As far as the data goes, and it has gone quite far since 1994, the trend never changes or gets reversed. The hyperbolic model that Lenski used to fit his data had an unfortunate characteristic. It had a fixed upper limit, meaning it predicted that fitness would not increase past a certain threshold, even if we were to wait for an infinite amount of time.

Twenty years later, the hyperbolic model was superseded by a power law model that had better predictive power and no upper bound, but, for a very long time, only the first hyperbolic model was used and referenced by other scientists. Whether there's a strong upper bound or not to any of these proposed models is not necessarily significant, as there's a limited amount of time available for evolution to work anyway. Even when that means millions of years, if a few decades can decrease fitness gains below 1%, the prospects of such extended time frames might not be as profitable as some would wish them to be. It is true that fitness is not equivalent to evolution, but it is an absolute requirement because, without an increase in fitness, natural selection would have a hard time creating a new, more-advanced organism. The lower the fitness gain is, the harder it is to select a mutated gene, and the less likely the gene will survive in a population full of genomes that lack the mutation. Even if a beneficial mutation gets selected, the next beneficial mutation will always be harder to find because, after each successful gain, the difficulty will increase until even millions of years are no longer sufficient to yield a beneficial mutation. Given how rapidly fitness gains are decreasing in the *E. coli* experiment, it is unlikely that we would have to wait long before the experiment reaches the point where we would not be able to measure any gains in fitness.

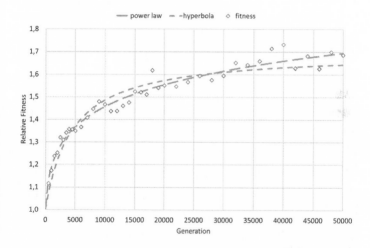

E. Coli Average Fitness

The observation of the fitness trends following the law of diminishing returns was not something that was necessarily expected in the experiment. This may sound unjustifiable because when there are no expectations, everything becomes unexpected, but that doesn't imply that some trends would not fit the hopes of evolutionary biologists more than others. There is no expectation in the theory of evolution that would require fitness to follow a particular trend curve. It could have gone in any number of different ways. We could have seen a much more uneven distribution of fitness in which gains could start sluggishly for some time but eventually pick up and attain high yields rather than continuously decelerating. For example, if a mutation opened up an evolutionary pathway that was previously unavailable and created novel machinery, that event could increase the fitness tenfold. However, such things were not observed. There was only a single event during the experiment that could be described as a novelty.

The contents of the vials used to grow the *E. coli* were pretty much standard for such experiments, except for the fact that the amount of glucose was decreased so that the bacteria would starve. This meant that there were other ingredients in the vials, substances that the bacteria could not normally consume. One of those substances was citrate, which the bacteria could not use to grow on but was, nevertheless, provided with in its standard experimental amount. *E. coli* can technically feed on citrate, but normally, it can only do so in an environment that is not rich in oxygen, and the vials had plenty of oxygen molecules to suppress the bacteria's ability to consume this food resource. Oxygen represses the expression of the gene responsible for creating the citrate-transporting molecules, thereby preventing the bacteria from growing on citrate. However, this blocking mechanism changed at around the 30,000th generation when the citrate started to disappear in one of the 12 vials, thanks to the bacteria gaining the ability to consume it. The trait itself was acquired when the citrate-transporting gene was duplicated, which moved it from the area that the repressor molecules could bind to, making the gene active despite being in an oxygen-rich environment. Whatever negative effect this might have had on the bacteria was overshadowed by the fact that now it could consume the relatively large amounts of citrate found in the vials.

This new discovery made quite a stir in certain circles. Nevertheless, the fact that E. coli has all the machinery necessary to acquire and process citrate did make the discovery somewhat lacking in terms of novelty so long as that detail was not omitted from the story. The citrate mutation did increase relative fitness for that single bacteria strand that was affected by it, but it wasn't any more exceptional than any of the other beneficial mutations were, as it couldn't even slightly bend the trend line of the fitness curve. As far as statistics are concerned, nothing out of the ordinary had happened. The only reason why this mutation was picked out from many other beneficial mutations was simply because it exerted an unusual impact on the environment that was visible to the researchers, while others were not. If the bacteria had managed to alter its glucose-processing machinery to make it compatible with citrate, then that would have been a feat to behold. Fifty-thousand bacteria generations were not sufficient for the remaining 11 bacteria strands to gain the ability to process the citrate located in the vials, even though such a change would have been clearly advantageous. How long would we need to wait for E. coli to be able to do that? Another 50,000, a hundred thousand, or perhaps a million generations? How steep would the fitness curve be after a million generations, if it followed its current trajectory? It would become almost completely flat. At that point, would natural or any other sort of selection be able to pick out a beneficial mutation if the benefit in fitness was less than a fraction of a fraction of 1%? If fitness gains are so meager that natural selection can't tell left from right, how could any kind of metabolic system possibly evolve? And, yet that seems to be the normal state of affairs in nature, so why do we believe that such systems have evolved repeatedly?

Evolution is often treated as an endless source of new

information in which every mutation sets up the necessary conditions for hundreds more, exponentially increasing the possibilities every time a beneficial mutation is fixed into the gene pool. We conceptualize evolution as if every evolving organism had hundreds of doors ready to be opened in the corridor leading to the next species, and each door led to new corridors with even more doors, giving the species even more possibilities to advance further each and every time a door was opened. It could be described as an endless cycle of progress that would grow exponentially. That is an interesting interpretation of the origin of species; however, the *E. coli* experiment suggests that evolution is only exponential in reverse. For every door it opens, even if that leads to new potential and new doors to open, it closes exponentially more and, therefore, closes more than it ultimately opens. This decreases the total number of doors available, which increases the time it takes to find one and that reduces fitness gains over time, which is exactly what we saw in the LTEE. Every time a beneficial mutation was found, it increased the time necessary to find the next one and that directly affected the fitness gains, constantly decimating it as time progressed and new generations were born. That is what the fitness data of the LTEE seems to suggest rather than the optimistic outlook of the endless potential of natural selection that many have subscribed to.

This issue can be solved or, at the very least, explained away by simply invoking the concept of fitness landscapes, which in all honesty could be an acceptable solution to this problem. In a fitness landscape, there are several fitness peaks that the organism, in this case the bacteria, can reach. Once reached, it might stay there for a while until some event, most likely a change in the environment moves it down from the peak, and the organism starts to ascend another peak while gaining new genetic information. This way, the organism can hop from peak to peak, which grants it an endless amount of potential to evolve new characteristics. As, in the *E. coli* experiment, the environment was static once it reached the local fitness peak, which happened quite quickly, it could not move away from the peak. If the bacteria were to be put into a new environment with different conditions, they could continue evolving and reach heights they could not reach in the experiment. The fitness landscape offers a plausible explanation for how evolution could continue while fitness gains are in decline, but that is probably not the conclusion that evolutionary biologists were hoping for. After all, that was not something anyone had predicted, and, if nothing else, in this scenario, the visuals were certainly not favorable for the theory of evolution. I will expand on the concept of the fitness landscape and its validity in a later chapter.

In 2009, around the time I first started researching evolution, a book by the famous evolutionary biologist Richard Dawkins on the topic of evolution, *The Greatest Show on Earth: The Evidence for Evolution*, was released, which I promptly bought. This was not the first book Dawkins has written on evolution, but this was the book he wrote explicitly to provide proof for the theory. It was an interesting book, and I used it as a kind of source of sources, as I reasoned that if anything could be deemed as evidence for evolution, Dawkins would include it in his book. As the theory of evolution doesn't really have a central argument and is more like an amalgamation of arguments, it was helpful to have a proper list of arguments from its most prominent advocate so that I wouldn't miss anything by being ignorant about their existence. Needless to say, Dawkins has written extensively about Richard Lenski's LTEE, including the growth in cell size and density over time and even discussing the evolution of aerobic citrate metabolism. He went as far as including graphs for the change in cell volume and fitness from the 1994 paper mentioned earlier: namely, two graphs for the increase in cell volume over 10,000 generations, one for the average change and the other for the change in each individual population. In addition, he included one graph that illustrated the change in fitness of a single strand over 2000 generations. The first two used a hyperbolic function for their models, while a step function was used to fit the fitness data. You might recall that I mentioned that it would be quite tough for the average observer to tell that the fitness gains had diminished simply by looking at the step function. This is because the function has four flat surfaces, from which the first two and the last two are almost equal in size. While it is true that the first two are shorter, it would require a leap of faith to think that the surfaces would increase in size over time from that information alone. And yet Dawkins only included the step model, even though, in the original scientific paper, the graph that showed the mean fitness data for over 10,000 generations was also included, and that graph clearly demonstrated that the fitness gains were diminishing. Furthermore, he included a total of three graphs from the same paper, but not the one that was most relevant to the theory of evolution.

One might ask why he didn't include the graph for the 10,000-generation mean fitness data? He included it for 2000 generations. Why? There's also another graph that, instead of mean fitness, shows the fitness data for each of the 12 strands individually. That is also missing from the book. The only graphs that go as far as 10,000 generations that he included were the ones that showed a change in the cell size. It would have been highly unexpected for an observer to see that the cell size could increase indefinitely rather than losing steam over time. In other words, it would have been quite unnatural if the cell size growth of a single-celled organism didn't have strong physical boundaries, so seeing diminishing returns in those graphs are not unexpected. Fitness, on the other hand, is a different story because it strongly correlates with the process of Darwinian evolution. The omission of graphs is a curious decision by the author. The fact that graphs that accurately demonstrate the general trajectory of the fitness are missing would not have been problematic if the book mentioned that the fitness gains had sharply declined after a few thousand generations. The closest Dawkins gets to mentioning this detail is when he states that a hyperbolic function could have also been used for fitting the fitness data, but at that point, he also mentions that he personally prefers the model that uses the step function instead. You would have to know your math quite well and read very carefully to realize what a fitting using a hyperbolic function could possibly mean for the trajectory of future fitness data. There's absolutely no way that Dawkins could have missed this detail, as Lenski alluded several places in the research paper to the fact that gains were in decline and the related graphs were quite damning as well.

The question here is why would Dawkins leave out this important information or any reference to it, be it textual or visual, from his book? I believe that he found something unsettling about these graphs and didn't want his readers to be burdened by the conclusions the datasets were implying. The point here is not that Dawkins was wrong to leave out this information but that it represented something that he specifically didn't like and did not want to show to others. Thus, it is interesting that I, from the very beginning, believed that the decline in fitness gains could potentially pose a problem for the theory of evolution and focused on the particular data points that Dawkins choose to omit. After all I would have never noticed the omission if that was not the case. I believe that we both found the data problematic and, in this one thing, Prof. Dawkins and I are most likely to have been on the same page for a very long time.

Of course, whether we agree on this point or not has absolutely no evidentiary value related to the question of whether the fitness data of the LTEE poses a problem for the theory of evolution or not. I merely wished to underline that my claim regarding the results of the Lenski experiment being neither predicted by biologists nor favorable for their theory has some merit. I had no intention to use this as a rhetorical argument for my opinion or to besmirch the reputation of a scientist, which is why I am making this clarification before I continue. If, however, you still believe I am guilty of any of the accusations I just mentioned, know that I am certainly not alone in this regard, especially if you consider how toxic this particular field of study has been to intellectual dissidents. While this fact may not excuse any perceived transgressions, it certainly makes me feel less remorseful for taking a detour from my main argument.

Whether the diminishing quantity of the fitness gain in the experiment supports or contradicts the theory of evolution is not something we can at present decide, but that doesn't mean that the scale isn't tipped to one side. It simply means that we can't see to which side the scale is tipped as if the scale itself was obscured in a room full of smoke, but if we could do some further investigation inside the room, we might learn which side of the scale has more weight to it. We can never know for certain, but perhaps we can know enough to make an informed guess on this matter. Science, after all, does not deal with certainty, only with probabilities, and whichever theory has the higher predictive power should weigh the most on our scale, regardless of its contents. Yet, to even attempt such a feat we must delve deep into some theoretical and possibly speculative arguments, which might not be able to meet the kind of scientific standards we should all strive for. Still, in hopes that one day these points may help someone reach those heights, I will lay out my arguments on this matter as best I can.

Chapter 6

Complexity in a Nutshell

A ll organisms in nature are based on the information encoded in DNA, and the evolution or change of that information is what drives speciation. Thus, the origin of species is tightly bound to the concept of information and to complexity as well. Any study of the origins must be able to explain the nature or content of the information located in DNA and the amount or complexity it has, and how it changes over time. To do this, we must understand what information and complexity really are.

Complexity is a difficult concept mostly because it is an attribute of nature that is not well understood and because there are several theories that provide different interpretations of the same concept. The idea itself is mostly tied to the field of computer science, but pretty much all science must use it in some form or another. Unfortunately, "complexity" has become a loaded word and is often ridiculed when it is used in the context of evolutionary biology. Once at a public lecture, a biology professor used the words "complexity" and "complicated" 23 times in about a minute, only pausing to let the audience laugh when describing his opposition's main argument. The concept and the arguments derived from it are frequently made fun of and, unfortunately, even more often ignored. However, as complexity is directly tied to the concept of information, which happens to be invaluable for the understanding of genetics, there can be no good reason to outright dismiss the concept. For better or worse, complexity differs from other attributes of stuff found in the universe, such as weight and length. There's no "real" way to measure it: no scale can weigh it, and no camera can record it. In some respects, it is more elusive than dark matter, as we can't accurately measure it even when it's right in front of our eyes. And, yet complexity must exist simply because information exists and because, by definition, the complexity of an object is the quantity of information contained in that object. Complexity is the answer to the question "how much information is in an object?" rather than "what kind of information does the object contain?" or, more simply, "what is the object?" Complexity is used to measure an object's quantity of information, in the same way as mass and weight is used to measure the quantity of matter in an object. Complexity is not the content itself; it can't tell you what the information is about, only how much of it there is. At least that is what we are hoping for, but because information is a somewhat difficult concept to grasp, complexity has become a somewhat elusive property.

If I would ask someone what is more complex: a random stone or a functioning mobile phone, each consisting of an equal number of atoms, most people would say that the phone is more complex. The question is, why do we think that? Or rather, could one devise a mechanical instrument, such as a scale or a ruler, that could confirm the proposition, and if not, why does anyone believe that one is more complex than the other? Can science confirm such statements? If it can't, isn't it just superstition? You see, this is where the true problem lies. If it is a superstition, what is its origin? What holy text, holy man, or unpredictable natural phenomena is responsible for it? If we were to ask 100,000 people that question, we could statistically verify that there's a clear bias toward choosing the mobile phone over the stone as the correct answer. There would probably be some who would say they are of equal complexity and maybe a few who would choose the rock, but no matter how many times you would repeat the experiment, the phone would win the popular vote every single time. At least that is what I personally would expect to happen, and if I am right, we would have to ask, what causes this bias? The most likely explanation is that we have an innate ability to recognize and understand objects and guess the quantity of information within them as a consequence of our rational faculty. Understanding an object's structure and qualities is the same as reading the information out of the object and, if we can do that, we can undoubtedly measure the quantity as well. You can think of this as something similar to sight but, rather than seeing with our eyes, we are seeing with our mind's eye. Furthermore, just as we don't need to understand how the eye works for it to work, neither do we need to understand how the mind's eye perceives things to use it to gain knowledge of our surroundings. It simply works, and it works in our subconscious just as most things related to perception does without us being aware of it. It is no doubt a complex process that the brain does without our knowledge and requires no conscious interference on our part for it to work.

It is of great benefit that the brain can do the heavy lifting for us, but not having any conscious oversight on the process has its disadvantages. The same way as our senses can be fooled, giving us incorrect images of our surroundings and create a false perception of the world, so too can our mind's eye be deceived. If we can't perceive the information contained in an object, then we might not be able to judge its complexity accurately, which could easily lead to errors in the process of measurement. Consequently, if we base a theory on errors, any conclusions we draw from our theory will most likely be mistaken as well. We might perceive one object to be less complex than another object, even though the exact opposite might be true. For example, if you were shown a motherboard of a computer full of all kinds of chips and gadgets, you might say that this piece of hardware looks really complex. As most tools that we use in our daily lives, such as doors, chairs, forks, and so on, are much less complex than modern computers, it is generally okay to call computers or their parts complex to imply that, in this regard, they are extraordinary. A component of a computer must be assembled in a specific way to be able to accomplish a particular task, and that specificity makes it and the computer complex. This being the case, unless you know a lot of computer hardware, you might not be able to tell a genuine motherboard, in which every part is connected deliberately, from a fake, which was assembled randomly. It is not hard to build a piece of hardware that only resembles an actual computer component but would not work because it mimics the look and not its functionality. If such a part were to be shown to layman, they would most likely guess its complexity to be equal to the complexity of the real thing, which would be incorrect. Therefore, we should not forget that our senses, including those that perceive information, are not infallible. However, we should also not forget that such issues can be mitigated by our conscious effort to overcome them. If we had a deep knowledge of computers, for example, we could tell if a part was fake or not or whether the arrangement of the chips on a board made any sense at all. This is how we can solve the issue of our senses being fallible: by using our reason to gain knowledge that is able to pick out the errors that our subconscious might have made. Even if our eyes are fooled, we can differentiate a mirage from reality if we are aware of its existence and have developed methods to tell the two apart. We understand what a mirage is, and we have the means to recognize it whenever or wherever it occurs, despite the fact that our eyes can't tell the difference between it and reality. The fact that we use the word "mirage" to describe something proves that we can identify a mirage, otherwise not even the word would exist because everything, including mirages, would be recognized to be part of reality rather than a reflection of it. If we couldn't separate a reflection from reality, then a human wouldn't be different from an insect that couldn't tell the difference between a window that is open from one that is not. If we can recognize a mirage as fake, we should also be able to recognize an object that contains far less information than it first appears to have.

Information is a tricky concept. It can mean different things in different contexts. The field of informatics, in particular, has seemingly gained a monopoly over the word, even though it is generally only concerned with a small subset of the information that's out there. The field focuses on what we call recorded information, which includes both the written word and our memories, as well as data that is consumed by computers. Genetic information also falls into this category, as DNA and its contents are, in essence, not that far from computer hardware and data. Recorded information requires an interpreter that can read and act upon the information that has been recorded and, thus, such information cannot exist in a vacuum. An interpreter or reader is always needed, and if one does not exist, then the record can no longer be classified as information. The same way a lock without its key cannot function, so too a book without a reader will lose its meaning, and just as a lock that cannot be locked is nothing more than a piece of metal, so too will an unreadable book be reduced to simple paper and ink. A book that's not being read at the moment could potentially be read in the future and, therefore, has potential information, but a book that was written in a language that no one can read or decipher has lost all of its prospects to be read and, as a result, stopped being a source of information.

Other than having the necessity of a reader to exist, which can be someone or something, it is also important for the recording to actually contain information that can be interpreted; this means that the recording must contain information about something and not just be something. No recorded information can exist without its equivalent existing somewhere in nature. A recording stores information about something and cannot exist on its own without referencing some things that exist. Thus, recorded information has to be referential, implying that it has to reference things that exist somewhere in some form. Even made-up stuff, such as works of fiction, must reference the real world to be understandable by readers. It is true that not all things we imagine exist, but all things are made up of parts that do exist. Our imagination doesn't create information, but rather rearranges it in a way that is unique and has never been done before. For example, if we take a lightsaber from the Star Wars universe, we can say that such an object does not and probably cannot exist in our reality. That is true, however, things such as light and sabers do, in fact, exist in our universe, not to mention the fact that all of a lightsaber's other attributes were borrowed from our reality as well. For example, a lightsaber has weight and length, and it exists in a specific place. It can be moved, and it can be broken. Even the blade part of the saber strongly resembles a laser, which is why it is sometimes called a laser sword. It is true that a normal laser would not usually have a limit to its extension in space, but that is an attribute that was borrowed from swords rather than from lasers. A lightsaber may have a unique arrangement of attributes, but its attributes aren't unique at all. Even our own imagination has its limits. We can only mix things that we have experienced, but at the very least we can mix them any way we wish. The important thing is that a record has to reference things that exist for it to be considered information, even if the sum of its contents doesn't exist in reality. Accordingly, recordings referencing things that no longer exist can also be properly considered information. The referential nature of recorded information is what separates a record from a random arrangement of parts. What differentiates a word from a random set of letters and a sentence from a random set of words is the fact that these things have some meaning for someone or something. Being referential is what makes something a recording because it references something that by its very nature contains information.

The fundamental form of information is simply things being the sum of their own attributes. Everything is a set of attributes that collectively comprise the thing and nothing else, and that means that everything contains the information of its own self. An airplane contains just as much or even more information than the plan that was used to make the plane. It is only natural that the fundamental and most common form of information is simply the stuff that exists. The information that exists in a record is derived from this fundamental form, and that is exactly why we can say that a record is information because it is a record of things that by their very nature contain information. An object and a complete record of an object contain the exact same information and, therefore, have the exact same complexity. This fundamental truth can be used to measure the complexity of any object, as the complexity of a record can be determined by counting its parts or measuring its length, in the case of data. That said, measuring complexity is never completely accurate. Even if we do it as best as we can, there will always be a margin of error that we cannot eliminate. Thus, measuring complexity is similar to other types of measurements used in science as they, too, are inaccurate to some extent, but that doesn't mean that their accuracy is necessarily the same.

Creating a record of something in a uniform language so that its complexity could be measured is an arduous task, and there's almost no way to determine if someone has succeeded or not. Even knowing what the margin of error is supposed to be is pretty much impossible. However, we should not forget that our own mind is particularly adept at determining the information content and complexity of any object. After all, when we look at an object, in our mind, a record will be created of that object, which we can use to compare the relative complexity of that object to other objects. The more we know, the more accurate our predictions should become and, while this methodology might not be accurate or generally useful in most cases, there may be a few cases where its use should at least be considered.

Some differences exist in various fields of study regarding what may or may not constitute information. In informatics, sometimes we call something information that isn't really, simply for practical reasons; this is mostly what differentiates information from data, as data doesn't really need to contain any information for it to be recognized as being data. For example, a random set of characters would be treated the same as the source code of an operating system. Recorded information is always special in that it matches a pattern, the pattern of the thing that has been recorded; this is not necessarily true for data. Data can contain things that match no patterns. A random number or a text made up of a random sequence of letters can't match any kind of pattern. By definition, a random sequence is a sequence that does not match a pattern other than itself, implying that a random recorded value cannot be considered information and will have very little complexity to speak of. Fundamentally, in informatics, a random value is treated as having the most amount of information a value can have, rather than having a negligible amount or none at all. This is because a random value cannot be compressed and, therefore, takes the longest time to transfer over a computer network, which makes the concept useful in determining the limits of the network. In informatics, this feature of randomness is what we generally exploit and, more often than not, use numbers that are difficult to compress in the place of actual random numbers. Generally, if we need a random number, we use a program called a random number generator (RNG), which, if configured properly, can create a number that is very close in principle to a real random number—called pseudo-random numbers. Conventional computers are a hundred percent deterministic and, thus, they can never generate truly random numbers. Most algorithms that require randomness often don't need true random numbers as such numbers can be substituted with pseudo-random numbers generated by RNGs. Generating pseudo-random numbers can be a difficult task and sometimes crucial programs, such as encryption algorithms, may fail if they can't generate numbers that are reasonably close to true randomness.

While random numbers are an integral part of informatics, they are used very selectively because they are in essence the exact opposite of what information is. Random numbers and objects have little to no complexity to speak of, which is a detail that must be considered if our task is to measure complexity of certain things that may or may not be related to random causes and effects. Other than being used for encryption, random numbers are also utilized in some databases. For each record in a database, a random value is chosen as its identifier and, as a result of this process, that random value stops being random because it now identifies something that exists. While any value could have been chosen to identify that specific record, once one is chosen, only that one specific value will be able to do that. This grants the randomly chosen value some complexity, because, as long as it can be used to find a record in the database, it can no longer be considered random because it has that one single function to find something. The information content of this value is still very low because finding a single record is the only function it has, and we can still replace it with other values if we really wanted to, as it is not an integral part of the record it identifies. True information cannot be altered like that. For example, a plan that defines the structure of an airplane cannot be substituted with a random plan because if we changed the plan, it would no longer be the plan for that specific airplane. Besides, a plan holds information even without the plane, but the identifier in a database, in contrast, is meaningless without the record it is tied to. While a random identifier has some complexity, which it inherits from the system it is used in, that complexity can only equal a small fraction of the complexity of the whole system.

If we treated randomness as if it had the same complexity that its specificity implies, then our understanding of information would be torn apart. As it is relatively easy to create a simple machine that produces an endless stream of random numbers, we could simply generate an amount that would surpass the information created by the efforts of all of humanity past, present, and future. Therefore, this device would contain more knowledge than we could ever dream of about absolutely nothing. Given how easy it is to generate randomness and how difficult it is to attain knowledge, we should never treat the two as equals. If we are not satisfied with pseudo-random generators to be used for our device, we could use a beam splitter to generate an endless number of zeroes and ones that, because of the principles of quantum mechanics, would be truly random. When a beam is split, there's a 50% chance the resulting photon will hit one detector and a 50% chance it will hit the other detector, thereby creating either a zero or a one. By concatenating the bits generated by this machine, we can create numbers of any size. Devices like beam splitters do, in fact, exist; they are called true random generators and are available for purchase in certain electronics shops. Hence, we have the means to create a device that can generate an endless stream of random nonsense.

When measuring complexity, one of the easiest ways we can fool ourselves is by not recognizing certain things as the product of random chance, which could inflate our complexity estimates by a significant amount. As random values are treated in informatics as having the highest information density of any transferable data type, if we can't find and eliminate their interference in the process of measuring things, our results will not be accurate. Given how common inherently random quantum effects are in our universe, differentiating between the results of random events and the deterministic effects of the laws of nature can be extremely challenging when measuring complexity anywhere in the cosmos. Even in the case of the theory of evolution, random mutations are not accountable for the creation of information and for the subsequent increase in complexity, as only natural selection can determine what mutation is beneficial, regardless of it being random or not. Random mutations are the ink that evolution uses to write into the book of the genome, but natural selection is the force that determines what words that ink is used for.

Random values and their derivatives may be the most likely to be confused with information, but it is not the only form of data that can be created without limit, subsequently creating the appearance of information where there is none. The easiest way to increase the size of data is through repetition. If you have a piece of recorded information you can simply repeat it, which would double the size required to store it on a disk. We can repeat any instance of recorded information as many times as we like but would that action increase the amount of information we possess? Would the complexity double or triple if we repeated the same data two or three times in a row? Recorded information is simply a reference, so repeating it will only repeat the reference and not the thing it is referencing, and so new information is not being created by getting itself repeated. Moreover, unlike random values, it is pretty straightforward to compress data that have some sort of repeating element. If we, for example, repeated the contents of a book five times, we could simply conserve data by defining how many times the book needs to be repeated before it is shown to anyone and only creating the final product when it is actually needed. What we would have to store is the text of the book and the number five and some metadata that conveys the information about what should be done with this number. Thus, a book that was repeated five times could be reduced close to a single book without losing any information in the process; therefore, the parts that were repeated did not constitute any significant form of information. Directly repeating data is the simplest way of inflating information, but it is not the worst offender when it comes to inflating complexity estimates.

On the surface, it might seem easy to recognize the repetition of information. However, combined with other obfuscation methods, the task becomes much more challenging. Repetition can be used to create sets that are both nonrandom and nonrepetitive. For example, by using a computer program, you could create a set of numbers in which every number is one plus the number that came before it. The numbers in such a set would not be repetitive, but rather the result of a repeating algorithm and, therefore, would not be as complex as it first may seem. In many cases, it is easy to recognize when something is the result of simple rules being applied repeatedly over and over; however, sometimes, the discovery of such rules is not so obvious. For example, it would be particularly challenging to derive a guiding rule from an image of a Mandelbrot set; therefore, it would be hard to determine the true complexity of an image depicting the set because of its complex geometric shape.

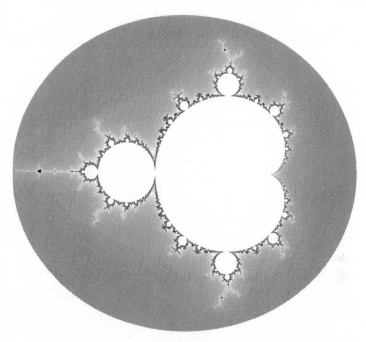

Mandelbrot Set

What if, for example, this picture was interactive, and you could zoom endlessly inside a computer program that would render new sections of the set on demand? Wouldn't that imply that the complexity of the Mandelbrot set is infinite? Processes that are infinitely repeatable and never-ending can create objects that are predominantly difficult to estimate when it comes to the question of their complexity. Unfortunately, in the cosmos, most things behave like that, and we must learn to cope with things of that nature; else, we can't hope to find estimates that are remotely accurate or useful. Our galaxy and solar system are governed by laws that change the attributes of the objects located inside them in an endless cycle of interactions, and the same is true for the elementary particles affected by quantum mechanics.

Owing to the nature of the universe, we cannot simply look at things as they are, but also as they were in the past, and we must work out how they have changed over time. We need to understand the process that changed them so that we may accurately judge their complexity. Hence, we are also interested in the process itself and not just its outcome. Measuring the complexity of any process can give more accurate estimates than trying to measure the object that was created by the process. After all, our world is not static, and any permanent object is somewhat of an illusion, as everything in our universe is, in truth, temporary in essence. Taking this approach will also be more useful because evolution is a natural process that is broadly believed to be still in progress. The complexity of a process may seem challenging to estimate, as everything involved in the process could be changing constantly, but there are ways to get around that problem. We need to answer the following question: what describes a process completely and has a finite non-changing quantity that we can measure? A program, or more precisely the source code of a computer program or algorithm, meets the criteria as long as the program is capable of creating the process and the object as the product of the process. If the program cannot create the process but can simulate it in a virtual environment, then our complexity estimates may still be accurate as long as the simulation closely resembles our own reality. There are processes such as the effects of the laws of nature that cannot be recreated but can be instead simulated virtually using computers. Scientists have created many virtual worlds to test quantum mechanics and the forces of nature, and, by looking at those algorithms, we may even be able to guess the complexity of the universe itself.

Therefore, the complexity of an object is equal to the

shortest algorithm that, if executed, will create the object. This value is called algorithmic complexity or, sometimes, Kolmogorov complexity, after the Russian mathematician who was one of the first to describe the concept in detail. Essentially, to know the complexity of a thing, we need to know the size of the algorithm that can create that thing. All things being equal, this would be the quantity of characters that compromise the text of the algorithm in question. Longer algorithms are more complex, while shorter are less, assuming that these algorithms are optimal solutions as far as their length in characters is concerned. Unfortunately, it is hard to know for sure whether a specific algorithm is, in fact, the shortest possible algorithm that could produce the desired results, simply because there's no way to determine that a shorter version does not exist. This is because a human is required to construct the algorithm, and no human can say for certain if an algorithm is, in fact, the shortest possible. At best, we can guess what the shortest possible algorithm might be, which adds a margin of error to our complexity measurements. Ultimately, what we can deduce is that the algorithmic complexity of an object will never be greater than the length of the shortest algorithm we have managed to find that is able to create it. It might be less, but it cannot be more. This adds a factor that is unfortunately very difficult to control; however, in many cases, acquiring an upper bound of complexity can be more than sufficient to answer questions regarding the plausibility of certain processes creating specific objects.

Algorithmic complexity is not necessarily the best way to measure the complexity of a process or an object, but it is definitely the most practical that can produce viable results in most cases. If, for example, we compare the complexity of two objects, as long as one is several orders of magnitude more complex than the other, then even algorithmic complexity should be capable of highlighting that difference. The utility of algorithmic complexity in biology should not be overlooked, as the contents of DNA, the genome, is essentially an algorithm that creates living organisms. Thus, as long as the length of the genome can be measured, we should be able to infer the complexity of any organism. This value conforms to our natural belief that single-celled organisms are less complex than multicellular organisms, as the former have generally shorter genomes compared with the latter. The correlation between genome size and complexity might seem self-explanatory, but, in truth, even that is not a trivial matter. Unfortunately, even DNA may be longer than it needs to be, so the complexity of some organisms might be much less than the length of their DNA; however, as long as such outliers are not the norm, algorithmic complexity can still be useful. Statistically, the more complex an organism appears, the longer its DNA will be; therefore, if we examine organisms that follow the general trend, it should be fine to use their genomes to measure their complexity.

One key consequence that must be mentioned about algorithmic complexity is that nothing, and I mean absolutely nothing, can be more complex than the algorithm that has created it. This fact can be easily deduced via reductio ad absurdum from the definition of algorithmic complexity. Imagine that you write an algorithm that creates another algorithm that is more complex than the initial algorithm. What would be the algorithmic complexity of this new algorithm? Based on the definition, it would be the length of the original algorithm or, at the very least, the complexity could not be more than the original's length. This implies that the complexity of the new algorithm would be less than that of the original and more than it at the same time, thereby leading to a contradiction. Consequently, the complexity of a product of any algorithm has to be less or equal to the length of the original algorithm. As long as we measure complexity in a way that is consistent with the idea of algorithmic complexity, this rule will remain absolute by logical necessity.

Evolution is a process that should be able to create new code and increase the complexity of living beings over time. Every natural process, including evolution, can be described by an algorithm; so, in theory, we should be able to write an algorithm that could potentially evolve life to higher levels of complexity. If we could create such an algorithm, we could compare that to the products of evolution and determine if one is more complex than the other. As the genome is essentially an algorithm and because it was produced by evolution, it cannot be more complex than the algorithm of evolution itself. Unfortunately, producing such an algorithm is virtually impossible because the simulation of natural selection would require at least the algorithmic equivalent of the sun, moon, and earth combined. Our planet, in particular, would be difficult to simulate because life as it evolves would greatly impact the state of the earth and, in turn, affect living organisms and the process of evolution. Even if we could write an algorithm of organic evolution, we will for sure not be able to run it in any meaningful way as software on a machine; so, we would never be able to tell if the simulation was representative of the process of evolution or not. This would make any comparison between the simulated algorithm and the products of evolution meaningless. However, that doesn't mean that the complexity measurements that we can gain by observing the genomes of different organisms could not be utilized in a different fashion. Organic evolution cannot be simulated, that is a fact; however, if we could create an approximation of the process of evolution, we might discover regularities that specifically correlate evolutionary algorithms as a set. Facts may exist that are true for all evolutionary algorithms for simply being evolutionary. If that is the case, it might not be necessary to simulate organic evolution with absolute accuracy, and even the greatly sought-after law of evolution might be within our grasp.

Chapter 7

Algorithm of Evolution

The modern theory of evolution provides a theoretical understanding of the process suggested by Darwin; however, if somebody wanted to understand evolution fully, he/she might need to write an algorithm that could simulate the process to see it during progress. Lexical knowledge is often mistaken for having a true understanding of a natural process, but someone who can create an accurate simulation of a particular phenomenon must have not only knowledge of but also a clear understanding of how the phenomena should work. The famous physicist Richard Feynman thought as much and, as his last words to his students, he wrote the following two phrases on his blackboard: "What I cannot create, I do not understand" and "know how to solve every problem that has been solved." Following Feynman's advice, I always believed that if I wanted to acquire an in-depth understanding of evolution, I would have to create something very similar to it that could be observed without waiting millions of years for any meaningful change to occur. When I started my research on the theory, the first task I undertook was to write an algorithm that could simulate the process in a digital space. As I had programming skills, this was a challenge I was more than happy to take on, even though I had no idea what I should expect from the end result.

To write a good evolutionary algorithm, I first needed to decide on a few rules for myself to follow. First, I wanted an algorithm with a graphical component so that others and I could visually confirm that it worked. Second, I wanted an algorithm that would run well on a single computer, as many others and I don't possess a supercomputer at home. Third, I wanted something that could be executed in an Internet browser so that I could easily share it with other people. Fourth, I wanted something that worked, something that could definitely create evolution inside a computer, something that would not fail to produce some result. This meant that I had to take any notion of the program being realistic or representative of natural selection and throw it out the window. Instead of attempting to mimic nature, I decided that simply imitating the conditions in which evolution would take place would be far more practical. As long as the fundamental rules were the same, it should not matter how much the details differed; after all, this algorithm is meant to facilitate a better understanding of the process and not create a representation of the real biological evolution. One reason for keeping it simple was so that I had less work to do; however, the main reason was that finding a problem that could be solved by an evolutionary algorithm is not as simple and straightforward as one might think, despite what evolutionary biology has been teaching us.

My evolutionary algorithm is as simple as they come. It has one polygon and, through the process of evolution, it morphs the polygon as close to the shape of a circle as computationally possible. It starts with creating a square somewhere in a digital space of a 500-by-500 two-dimensional plane. The square polygon has four points, of course, and each point is represented by two coordinates. This is the initial state of the algorithm before any mutation has occurred. So far, it's pretty simple, right? When the program starts, it goes into an iterative loop, and each iteration of the loop runs a specific set of actions on the square or whatever polygon it has mutated into. First, a random number of points is generated with random coordinates, which then gets added to the polygon at a random position between two existing points of the polygon. A random number of points is removed from the polygon in the same position where the new ones are inserted, so the new points might replace some of the old points; however, they might also be purely incremental without removing any points from the polygon. It is also possible that no new points are added while, some of the old points are removed, effectively decreasing the number of points in the polygon. Any randomly generated value can be zero, so adding zero new points and removing zero old ones are both possible. These additions and subtractions from the points of the polygon are the mutations that give our evolutionary algorithm the ability to change its own state. All that I mentioned up to this point, which takes care of the process of mutation, occurs inside a single iteration of the loop, and the iterative part cannot be complete with that alone, as we need a second component for evolution, which is selection.

In the environment, natural selection decides what survives and what does not; however, in a simulation, we must define the conditions that determine which specimens or, in this case, which polygons, are fitter than others. The conditions used for our selection process must be set such that they would facilitate the type of evolutionary progress that Darwin would expect to be responsible for the growth of complexity in nature. In other words, the level of complexity found in the system must increase as a result of selection and, as we know based on the last chapter what is and what isn't complex, we must be careful when choosing the right type of evolutionary algorithm. Lucky for me, I already had a good idea of what I should choose from the get-go. For some reason, the idea of generating circles from simpler polygons popped into my head as soon as I started working on the project. If you think about it, what is a circle, if not a polygon with an infinite number of points in a specific order and in precisely defined locations? That meets the definition of complexity; so, what I could do is start with a square, mutate it, and, if it becomes a polygon that more closely resembles a circle than its predecessor, I will keep the mutated specimen. Else, I would throw it away and continue with the old one. As the more points a polygon has, the closer it can resemble the shape of a circle, it follows then that if one starts with four points, evolution would increase the number to five and six and then seven and so on, thereby increasing the complexity of the system in the process. The only problem I had to solve was how to program a computer to test if one polygon looked more like a circle than another.

Determining the "roundness" of an object is, actually, quite easy, if you think about it in terms of the relationship between a circle's area and perimeter. A circle is a simple polygon with the largest area surrounded by the shortest perimeter. In mathematical terms, this would be A/P, or A/P^2 to be more precise. Let's call it the "geometric roundness value" or "roundness" for short. The roundness value can be easily calculated by a computer or even by a human, especially if the polygon has a regular shape. For example, a square's area is equal to the square of its side (a^2), and its perimeter is equal to four times its side ($4a$), which if squared would be 16 times its side squared ($16a^2$). If we divide these two numbers $a^2/(16a^2)$ we get one divided by 16 or 0.0625 in decimals. This is the geometric roundness of any and all squares, which means that this value is a constant for any polygon that has the shape of a square, regardless of the size or position of the polygon. What is the geometrical roundness value of a circle, though? If we are discussing a perfect circle that we could not define as a polygon, because it would require an infinite number of points, we could still use its circumference to do our calculation. The area of a circle is PI multiplied by the square of the radius of the circle (πr^2), and its circumference is two times PI multiplied by the radius ($2\pi r$). Squaring the circumference would give use four times PI squared, multiplied by the square of the radius ($4\pi^2 r^2$). Dividing the area of a circle and the square of its perimeter gives us the number one divided by four times PI ($1/4\pi$) or 0.07957747, and so on in decimals. As the circle is the most geometrically round shape possible, no shape can have a greater roundness value than the circle. One-fourth of PI is the maximum that any polygon can theoretically possess; however, that value would require an infinite number of points, so it is impossible, in practice, though getting very close to this maximum is still very much in the realm of possibility.

The area and perimeter of any simple polygon can be easily calculated by a computer, and the roundness values of these polygons can be derived from these two values. Thus, when a new polygon is created at the beginning of the next iteration of our loop, we can quickly generate the geometric roundness of this new shape. We can compare this new value with the roundness value of the old polygon and, if this new value is greater than the old, then we can replace the old polygon with the new and continue the loop by beginning the next iteration, which would use the new polygon as its baseline. If the new polygon doesn't have a greater roundness value, then the old polygon is kept, and the new is thrown out. This way, the geometrical roundness value of the polygon can only go up, and the only way it can go up is by acquiring new points that mutate the polygon to align better with the shape of an ideal circle. As we are starting with a square that has four points and a roundness value of 0.0625, there's considerable room for both the number of points and the roundness value to increase significantly. Even in a limited space of a 500-by-500 two-dimensional plane, many potential points exist that the evolutionary algorithm can incorporate into the structure of the evolving polygon.

There are many ways to calculate the exact area and perimeter of a simple polygon using mathematically proven algorithms. Some are better than others, but ultimately the slowest method is sufficient to generate good results. I have optimized my evolutionary algorithm over the years, but ultimately no change made any meaningful difference. The program did not get considerably faster nor did my calculations get a lot more precise as a result of any of my enhancements. Surely, if I had run my program for a year instead of a few minutes, considerable time would have been saved if I used an optimized algorithm, but such a long test seemed unnecessary to prove any point I wished to consider. Moreover, I must confess here that I only evolved a single specimen instead of a number of specimens, as the latter would have required much more resources to execute and considerably more effort from me. If I had a server farm in my backyard, it would have made sense to run code in parallel, but without it, linear execution is the most sensible choice. Whether it is one specimen evolving for a thousand generations, or a thousand specimens evolving for one generation, in the grand scheme of things, it will not make much of a difference. The only drawback of sequential evolution using a single specimen is that the number of generations gets inflated by a considerable amount. For example, if we had a population that numbered a thousand specimens, then that population would evolve as much in a thousand generations as a single specimen would do in a million. Thus, if we wanted to know how many generations it would take for a population of a certain size to evolve to the same level as our lonely specimen, then we would have to divide the number of generations of the latter with the population size of the former. As I never intended to use the number of generations that my algorithm would require to reach any conclusion of great importance, it did not make sense to care about whether the actual number was inflated or not. Generating circle-like polygons with a computer is not representative of biological evolution anyway, so it is meaningless to care about the number of generations required to produce any of the results. It is a simulation of the process, not a simulation of life evolving on Earth.

I have run my circle evolution program many times, and generally it has always produced the same results. Starting from a four-sided polygon, it quickly adds points to the shape and then alters the locations of those points so that they fall closer to the boundary of the circle the algorithm has selected accidentally. The results of different tests have been consistent with each other, or at least as consistent as can be excepted from an algorithm continuously generating random numbers. The curve of the roundness value of the polygon would shoot up at the beginning but quickly level off as it got closer to the maximum of $1/4\pi$ or 0.07957747. In a limited digital space, the ideal circle cannot be drawn, so this maximum is impossible to reach, but a polygon that is a close approximation of such a circle can be created. A mathematician could calculate the best possible arrangement of points, given a space with a definite width and height, but because I am not a mathematician, I opted for a simpler solution commonly known as brute force in the IT industry. I wrote a program that generated regular polygons repeatedly, then increased the number of points it included and its radius until the highest roundness value inside the two-dimensional space was found. Creating regular polygons is quite simple, so it takes the algorithm less than a second to find the best possible candidate. In my case, that polygon had the roundness value of 0.07953140, so only 0.00004 less than the ideal of $1/4\pi$. That roundness value is reached by generating the largest possible approximation of a circle limited by the constraints of the two-dimensional space set by the algorithm in advance.

I have run my evolutionary algorithm many times, and one thing became clear quite quickly: while every run would generate a polygon that would seemingly take the shape of a circle, these circle-shaped polygons differed from each other in one crucial aspect. The randomly generated points meant that the positions of the newly created points were always different, and that much is to be expected; however, the biggest difference between the circle-like shapes generated by the algorithm was the high variability in their diameters. While some had a diameter close to the boundary of the digital space the polygon was allowed to occupy, others were closer to half of that distance. Most were not very small, probably, because the initial polygon was also not small; however, the difference between the largest and smallest generated polygons was very noticeable. This variability was also the result of the randomly generated coordinates. At the start of the algorithm, many beneficial mutations could be found, signifying many valid points that could be added to the polygon, and some of these points were closer to the edge of the two-dimensional space than others. Every time a valid point is found, it reduces the set of possibilities, and what remains is geometrically located closer to the existing points of the polygon, and to the points of the circle that would best fit the current shape of the polygon. Thus, a few points found far from the center would make it much more likely that the next point would be found closer to the boundary of the space, while a few points found closer to the center would make it less likely for the same points to be found near the boundary. This way, the more points the polygon has that seems to favor a certain radius, the more likely the next point will also favor that radius, which, if found, would further increase the probability of the same cycle repeating. This is a self-strengthening process, so if some points were found by the algorithm that favor the same radius, then the polygon will be trapped, and the program will only be able to create the circle tied to or near that radius.

Circle-shaped polygons are not created equal, and larger ones can evolve longer and attain better roundness values than their smaller counterparts. When the algorithm starts, however, this small detail has almost no effect on the progress of the evolutionary process. Luck decides whether a circle will grow big or not. It might seem that an increase in the population size could remedy this issue, which is true to some degree. All things being equal, larger polygons have more beneficial mutations to choose from, but the main factor, even for a large polygon, would be chance and not whether a circle is closer to the optimal size or not. A large population size would skew the results toward more optimal results, but to reliably reach the most optimal size would require a population that is astronomical in size. Without that, we would most likely obtain a suboptimal result and, the longer it evolves, the less likely it could be anything but suboptimal. With every new generation, the chance of the polygon reaching the optimal size decreases because optimization requires the creation of the same number of points in a single generation as the polygon at that moment had, all with the right coordinates and in the right order, but with a higher roundness value to change the radius of the polygon. As gaining a new point or altering an existing one is a lot easier than replacing the whole polygon with a better one, the evolutionary process itself prevents the polygon from reaching its optimal size. This is an evolutionary barrier that cannot be broken within realistic bounds and, if a simple algorithm like this has such limitations, one might wonder what constraints biological evolution might possess.

As my tests produced roughly the same results each time I ran it, I randomly chose one for closer inspection. This test ran for one million iterations, taking 48 seconds to complete. The roundness value increased from 0.065 at the first to 0.07921792 at the one-millionth generation, and the polygon grew from 4 points to 49 points. A total of 139 beneficial mutations had been found in the one million mutation attempts generated by the algorithm.

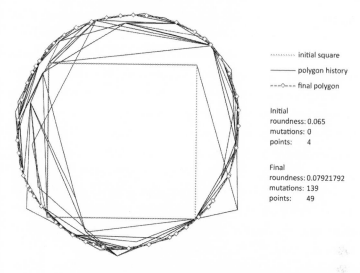

Circle Evolution 1 Million Generations

The polygon area increased by about 80%, while its perimeter also increased, but only by 20%. Plotting the round-ness values of different generations on a graph revealed that while the increase in roundness was promising initially, it declined sharply in later generations. If we consider the initial polygon to be equal to 100%, then in the first 200,000th generations, roundness increased by 26.32%, in the second by 0.25%, in the third by 0.11%, in the fourth by 0.05%, and in the fifth by only 0.01%. In other words, roundness followed the law of diminishing returns by decreasing the amount of change exponentially over time. This should come as no surprise because there are both theoretical and practical limits to the maximum value an evolving polygon could potentially reach. That said, in an ideal world, the roundness value could technically increase forever, even if it could not increase above a specific threshold. A computer would eventually run out of points it could find if only natural numbers were allowed as valid coordinates for the point or decimal places. Even if fractions were allowed, it would take a very, very long time to reach the final state. To the casual observer, it would seem that the sequence of growth would continue forever, even though it was greatly constrained from the get-go.

The shape of the trend curve of the roundness values is quite remarkable. As in a computer simulation we have every single value of every single generation, we can construct a curve that is 100% accurate, something that is not possible in different types of experiments. There are no margins of errors in a simulation if it is run correctly. In our case, the artificial randomness of our pseudo-randomly generated values is the most likely source of bias altering our algorithm; however, for the sake of argument, we will treat them as true random values and ignore the possibility of the artificial randomness having any effect on the outcome. After all, these same random numbers are used to encrypt the Web, so it would not be normal to expect them to have significant bias, at least not when so few as two million are generated. Therefore, our numbers must be extremely accurate, and only the size of our graph will diminish the precision of their values; after all, putting a million generations on any graph will result in some loss of data. Fortunately, plotting the values on a 500-by-500 coordinate system can accurately illustrate the story of the program. We know that, over time, the roundness value decreases exponentially, but the distribution of the diminishing returns is not equal over different time periods. In the beginning, evolution is much quicker than in later generations because it is much easier for the algorithm to find beneficial mutations when there are much more to choose from rather than when that number has greatly diminished. Besides, while the algorithm is looking for a new or better-positioned point, the shape will remain unchanged, creating a flat surface in the trend curve for that period. These flat surfaces grow in length over time because of the shortage of beneficial mutations, which result in a step-like trend curve with progressively elongated steps.

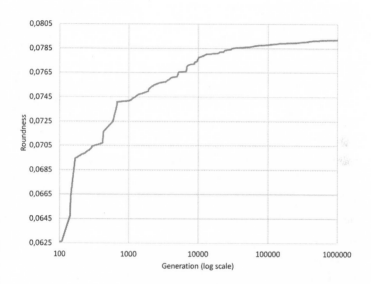

Circle Evolution Roundness

If you have read Chapter V recently, all of these facts should sound very familiar to you. A shape similar to that of a step function and exponential regression of values is the exact same pattern that has been observed in the long-term evolution experiment (LTEE). When comparing the graphs of relative fitness from the LTEE and roundness curve from the circle evolution, one can simply not tell which is which, if not because one is much more detailed than the other because it is a simulation. Although the roundness value of the circle algorithm is meant to measure complexity rather than fitness, it also reflects fitness gains, as complexity cannot increase without fitness. Therefore, we can treat roundness as being representative of the polygon's fitness, which if we do, should alter how we look at the fitness measured in the *Escherichia coli* (*E. coli*) experiment as well. The roundness value a polygon can achieve by evolving has a hard limit, which while it would take an infinite number of generations to reach, nonetheless gets very close, very quickly. If this is how a simulation of evolution can work, then shouldn't we expect evolutionary experiments to work the same way, if they give the exact same results as our simulation did? Remember that in the LTEE, a power law function was used to model the progression of fitness and that function, unlike the previously used hyperbolic model, did not have a limit other than infinity. That model must be incorrect and will become worse as new data are generated; at least, that is my expectation. You can also call it a prediction, but unfortunately it might take a few decades before my hunch can be verified. This is the long-term evolution experiment (LTEE) we are theorizing about, after all.

The circle algorithm seems to confirm the assertion that, in the LTEE, the complexity of the bacteria has increased through the process of evolution; this is, indeed, a possibility, but we must be really careful if we wish to make such a far-reaching statement. It is true that, *E. coli* has gone through some form of evolution in the LTEE. This process might not have exactly been natural evolution, but it was nevertheless something very similar to it, something that should be analogous to the real thing. This much we can say is a fact, but whether complexity has increased over the duration of the experiment is a different question. Is it possible that the bacteria did not increase its complexity during the LTEE, despite the fact that its fitness data were remarkably similar to that of the circle evolution algorithm? First off, remember that the circle evolution algorithm that we compared the LTEE to was designed to imitate how scientists believe evolution should have taken place and not to accurately simulate it. I had to carefully choose the problem I needed to solve with my algorithm so that my program would be guaranteed to succeed. My only requirement for the algorithm was that it had to increase the complexity of the thing that was evolving, but that requirement did not exist in the LTEE. The circle algorithm was designed to increase the number of points of a polygon and increase the accuracy of coordinates of the generated points, thereby increasing complexity. Hence, what happens to the circle algorithm if the incremental complexity of the polygon is treated as a detriment for evolutionary progress? What happens when destroying complexity becomes favorable instead of being harmful?

Reversing evolution in the circle algorithm is not a difficult task. We just need to change the selection criteria from favoring high-roundness values to disfavoring them, meaning that any new generation with a lower-roundness value will be kept, while every other will be discarded. Because we started with a simple square in the original algorithm, it is necessary to increase the complexity of the starting polygon so that more of it may be removed by the algorithm. I used the shape created by the algorithm that was tasked to find the most circle-like polygon that could be created in our limited digital space, which of course has, as a consequence, the highest roundness value and complexity. This polygon has a lot of complexity it can lose when the rules get reversed. We can call this the anti-circle algorithm, which instead of generating the largest area with the shortest border, will produce shapes with the smallest area and longest borders. The polygons this algorithm generates are more diverse than the original algorithm, but they tend to have few points with very sharp edges and as little surface area as any shape can allow. Naturally, if starting from a circle-like shape with lots of points, most of them will be deleted, and the rest will be moved around to reduce the area of the polygon. Rather than gaining points, this algorithm favors the loss of points—at least at the beginning—which differs from the original algorithm, but the shape of the new fitness curve remains remarkably similar to the original. There are only so many points that can be removed or moved around to produce the sharpest polygon imaginable before the evolution of this polygon will begin to stagnate as well. The same fitness curve of diminishing returns and step-function-resembling shape is seen in the anti-circle algorithm as we could find in the circle algorithm and the LTEE. Simply by looking at the fitness graphs, one cannot tell the difference between constructive evolution in which complexity is gained and destructive evolution in which complexity is lost.

There is only one way to tell which algorithm creates and which destroys complexity, and that is by putting the fitness curves of both the circle and anti-circle algorithms on the same graph. While it is true that both algorithms produce the same shape, the speed at which they produce them is quite different. The anti-circle algorithm is several orders of magnitude faster at destroying information than the original can create it, and this fact becomes more apparent when we check the change in the number of points for both polygons and the speed at which they are gained or lost. The time it takes to find a point is around a thousand times slower on average than it is required to remove one. This should come as no surprise because destruction doesn't need to be as selective as construction, as removing a specific point from the polygon is much more likely to happen than for the same point, with the same coordinates, to be added at the correct place in the list of points. Thus, the clearest giveaway for destructive evolution is the observation of direct loss of raw complexity. This is a key point that must not be forgotten because so much of the modern theory of evolution rests on the presupposition that fitness leads to evolution. And it does, as a matter of fact; it just does not always lead to the kind of evolution that can create more complex organisms. In reality, evolution by construction and evolution by destruction happen simultaneously, but if one is favored by the environment over the other, then the favored will dominate to an extent that the other will be barely noticeable. This was the case in the algorithms we are discussing and, by changing our selection criteria, we could easily change the evolutionary process from construction to destruction.

A crucial question we must ask to differentiate destruction from construction is: what can change the selection criteria in nature? What changes natural selection? The answer to that is whatever defines the selection criteria and, in the case of natural selection, that is the environment the organism lives in. If the environment changes, so does natural selection, and that could easily lead to either a more constructive or more destructive evolution. If we take a look at the concept of the fitness landscape, then we can see that the change in the environment creates the possibility for both types of evolutions. When an organism is introduced to a new environment and is pushed from the hill of a local optimum on the fitness landscape, then it is natural that, to adapt, it might need to incorporate new features to increase its chance of survival. This leads to constructive evolution. How fast this change will be and to what extent it can change the organism is up for debate, but some change will most likely occur to whatever extent it may be possible. Unfortunately, at the same time, some features that the organism possessed might become redundant or harmful as well. The organism cannot choose how its environment should change, so it is just as likely that the change would lead to its own degradation as it is to its advancement. If moving from peak to peak on the fitness landscape leads to the same amount of construction and destruction, then the organism will stagnate, which could mean that any movement on such a landscape is meaningless. If such an equilibrium is likely to exist in nature, then we could still have new species rising through evolution, but they would not be more complex than their ancestors, which is not how evolution by natural selection is supposed to work.

It is challenging to determine which type of evolution occurs in nature or how much of which type has taken place in the past. We simply cannot observe either, and we cannot determine it by trying to derive it from any kind of fitness data. What we do know is that destruction reduces complexity and that it tends to happen much faster than construction. These are signs that we can detect in an experiment; not necessarily both, though finding one would automatically presuppose the other. In the LTEE, both fitness and the raw complexity can be and has been determined, thanks to Lenski and his team. We know what the relative fitness in the LTEE was like, but we cannot compare it with any other fitness data, so we cannot determine if the speed of evolution was fast or not. In contrast, the raw complexity of the E. coli bacteria and the change that it underwent throughout the experiment can be discovered with effort. In the circle experiment, the number of points in a polygon was indicative of the raw complexity, but to determine the same value in the LTEE, a different kind of approximation is required. The easiest way to determine an organism's raw complexity is by calculating the size of its genome. The genome is an algorithm that produces the process of life and, therefore, the size of the genome should be equal to an organism's algorithmic complexity. This value is only an approximation, but if we are only interested in the raw complexity, which does not consider the question of how much simpler the object or function in question could be, then it's more than sufficient for the task at hand.

In a 2016 *Nature* paper, the researchers answered how much, on average, the genome of the *E. coli* bacteria has grown or shrunk in the first 50,000 generations of the experiment. According to the paper: "After 50 thousand generations, the average genome length declined by 63 kbp ($\sim$1.4%) relative to the ancestor." This implies that the bacteria lost 1.4% of its genome in only 22 years. Such a small loss might not seem much, but if this trend were to continue, then the bacteria would lose all of its genetic information in around 1500 years. It would be difficult to claim that the evolution in the LTEE was not predominately destructive in nature. In light of the evidence, this seems to be the truth, and it would be difficult to argue for the opposition. Of course, as usual, there were no expectations for the outcome of this particular experiment and for the results of the paper, but I would nevertheless argue that an increase in the genomic length would have supported the theory of evolution more than what was actually found. Meanwhile, it would be difficult to argue why anyone should have expected the length of the genetic material to increase in this experiment. After all, the experiment drastically changed the environment of the bacteria, which would have naturally rendered some of its genetic data obsolete. Consequently, that code had to be removed or deactivated and that is exactly what happened. In light of the havoc evolution has wrought on these bacteria, we must recontextualize the fitness data that the experiment produced. As destruction tends to produce the same fitness values in a fraction of the time that construction can, the 67% change in relative fitness during the first 50,000 generations in the LTEE is much less remarkable than it first seemed. In nature, such change would not happen unless some cataclysmic event occurred and, even then, such evolution could never produce more advanced life forms owing to its self-deprecative nature.

It has been said many times that evolution can only increase complexity and never decrease it. Technically this is true, as what destroys complexity is not evolution, but the movement or transfer of organisms from one environment to a different one. Evolution merely removes the obsolete information from the genome, making the operation of the organism more efficient, which naturally increases fitness. The information removed is at that point in time only noise and, by removing it from the genome, the specificity of the data would increase, which would increase its complexity as a result. In relative terms, that is relative to the organism's environment, evolution will never destroy the information located in the organism's genome. However, in absolute terms, which I define as relative to all environments of present and past, evolution can destroy information. To create more advanced life forms, evolution must increase the absolute complexity of organisms and not reduce it.

For unicellular bacteria and archaea to become multicellular and then become insects, plants, and animals, evolution must increase the amount of genetic information on Earth itself, and it has to do so by a considerable amount. The oldest known bacteria fossil is 3.5 billion years old, which belonged to an organism called *Cyanobacteria*. Earth is only 4.5 billion years old, so these bacteria have been around for well over half of Earth's existence. At present, *Cyanobacteria* have about three million base pairs in their genome and, for bacteria of this complexity to evolve into something like a human, it has to integrate an incredible amount of information into their

DNA over the years. The average human possesses three billion base pairs, and that amount is not extreme compared with the genomic size of other organisms. For an organism to acquire three billion base pairs in 3.5 billion years, it would have to gain on average 0.8 base pairs per year. Any number of base pairs lost in the process would have to be replaced and, at the same time, eight base pairs would have to be added every 10 years. That is the only way evolution can produce the things we see in nature and, fortunately for us, both time and the genomic size of organisms are things we can measure. If there is a law of evolution, it would have to be that genetic information has to increase on average at a rate equal to the genetic expansion rate of the past 3.5 billion years. This law fulfills all the scientific requirements needed for the theory of evolution to become an actual scientific theory. A true theory of science is one that can be falsified by comparing its predictions to nature and that is what this law can provide to the theory.

Measuring the genomic size of creatures that have died millions or billions of years ago can be a difficult task. The fossil remains of animals, insects, and plants from the past 500 million years do not contain much, if any, genetic data. That said, there are many species that have stayed the same for hundreds of millions of years, so we can make some guesses regarding their genomic complexity. We know when they first lived because of the fossil record, and we know what their genome is, if they are still around. In addition, we know of many bacteria that are billions of years old, so we have plenty of data to work with. One issue arises from the fact that complexity measured by the size of the genome is not always what we think it should be. Some organisms, especially plants, can have extremely long genomes, much longer than of any animal living today, and the same is true for amphibians, which tend to have long genomes as well. These categories include the genetically most complex organisms, but they also include beings that have several orders of magnitude fewer base pairs in their genomes. This is sometimes referred to as the C-value enigma in biology because there really isn't a simple explanation for it in the theory of evolution. The enigma poses a problem for validating any law of evolution based on the genomic length, but the issue can be minimized by focusing on certain subgroups in the main categories of organisms. For example, if we concentrate on the simplest groups of each main category, then there will be no C-value enigma to speak of. Amphibians will be less complex than mammals, and plants less complex than amphibians, and so on. The lower end of each category seems to coincide with evolutionary expectations and, as more complex organisms were preceded by less complex beings in the same category, this approach might be legitimate. Either way, there should be nothing preventing statisticians from working out a way to generate a representative dataset that could be used to validate this law of evolution.

I have previously alluded to the possibility that a law of evolution would be possible to construct based on the knowledge we already possess. The law I propose in theory fulfills the requirements that a historical science, such as evolution, must meet. Based on the uniformitarian approach of Charles Lyell, which supposes that natural phenomena of the past must be explained by causes now in motion, we too must look at the present to explain the evolutionary past. Just as the height of a volcano can be measured and be used to confirm the theory that it grows slowly over time, so, too, can the complexity of organisms be measured to possibly prove that organisms evolve slowly over time. This is Lyell's criteria for what constitutes good historical science, and this is also what

Darwin would deem good science, as he copied his own methodology from Lyell himself. Darwin simply attempted to apply it in biology instead of in geology, which was something Lyell seems to have been in favor of as well. Both men tried to solve the same scientific problems, though in different fields, and both ultimately built their science on John Herschel's philosophy. Remember that Herschel approved of Lyell's geology but harshly criticized Darwin's theory of evolution, even though Herschel was not, in principle, against a law of speciation. Even the phrase "origin of species" can be traced back to Herschel and, though Darwin really wanted his support, Herschel never accepted Darwin's theory. Herschel believed that a law of speciation must meet two simple criteria: direction and extent. In the case of the law of evolution, this would imply that complexity must increase over time, which fulfills the criteria of direction, and complexity must change by a specific amount that is consistent with prediction, which fulfills the criteria of extent. Thus, the law of evolution, which is neither a law of variation, nor a law of fitness or even of natural selection, fulfills all the objective scientific criteria derived from the philosophy of science that no other idea in the theory of evolution has managed to do before.

The work required to prove the law of evolution may be challenging, but it is not impossible, and, while no answer derived from any such study will be without error, we should ask ourselves: should we base our views on possibly incorrect data or on no data at all? Assuming, of course, that the law of evolution will prove and not falsify the theory, which seems to be just as probable, in my opinion. I will not be the one who does the work to validate this law. It is not my duty to make evolution a proper science; I merely wish to highlight that it is indeed possible, even if there's nobody who is willing to do it. The burden of proof lies with those who make a claim, and rejecting this burden or simply ignoring the absence of proof will not make the problem disappear. The issues of Darwin's theory have been with us since its inception, and the only difference between today and back then is that Darwin did not have the means to solve these problems, but we do.

Chapter 8

Evidence for Anecdotes

The theory of evolution, like geology, requires a specific form of proof, but because such endeavors lack any interest or even acknowledgment of their necessity, we don't possess rigorous proof for the theory. In its absence, less viable arguments have been used to support Darwin's theory. Many such arguments are based on anecdotal evidence, which in science is defined as: "Based on casual observations or indications rather than rigorous or scientific analysis." For simplicity sake, I treat any observation that is not a measurement an anecdote, and any argument from such an observation, an anecdotal argument. While these arguments have some merit, they lack the scientific rigor of a proper theory and are not as persuasive as they are claimed to be. Or at least they shouldn't be, given how much of the evidence rests on these informal anecdotes. Such facts can be still treated as evidence, but without measurements to do and projections to falsify, there can be no question that these arguments are of a lesser quality than one would normally find in science. Darwin tried very hard to not rely on such arguments in the *Origin of Species*, probably because he realized that was not the right way to establish a new science. It is unfortunate that, since then, anecdotal evidence has become the main source of proof, which has profoundly transformed the landscape of evolutionary thought. Anecdotes are usually impossible to falsify, but nevertheless can rest on facts that can be verified, which can make it seem that the theory is based on facts, but, at the same time, prevents the possibility of critique. Relying on such rhetorical argumentation would undoubtedly freeze progress in any kind of science, and evolutionary biology doesn't seem to be an exception. The theory reached its zenith and became stagnant the moment these arguments became mainstream.

Perhaps, it would be best to show through an example why anecdotal evidence is an unreliable way to develop any kind of science. Let us consider Newton's law of gravity and Einstein's theory of relativity for a moment. Both theories explain the movement of planets. Newton's law was first and, at the time of its inception, a very accurate hypothesis. You could predict where a planet would be seen in the future on the night sky; however, after a while, some discrepancy was discovered between the measurements and the law. Some objects in space did not move as had been predicted. The discrepancy was eventually solved by Einstein's theory of relativity, which was considerably more complex than Newton's law. Both theories explained how planets moved in the sky, but one was more accurate than the other and so the theory of relativity prevailed. Now, consider the possibility that we can't or don't want to make accurate measurements. How would we be able to tell which theory is the best? What if all the proof we had was based on anecdotal evidence? For example, consider the claim: Newton's law predicts that planets will move in an ellipsis. We can check if that is true, and it is, which means that Newton was right. Or more formally: I observe that planets move in ellipses, and Newton's law predicts that planets move in ellipses; therefore, Newton's law is correct. This way we can get an argument from an anecdote without the need to compare any predictions to measurements. Likewise, Einstein's theory predicts that planets follow the curve of an ellipsis when they move, so which one is correct? This is when a philosopher of science can help the situation. As he can't make any measurements himself, what he can do is to suggest the use of Occam's razor to solve the dilemma. Occam's razor states that, all things being equal, the theory that makes the least unnecessary assertions is probably the correct one. In other words, the simpler the theory the better, and relativity is anything but simple, so Newton must be the winner here and not Einstein. I am hopeful that this thought experiment has demonstrated why informal anecdotes in science are often not sufficient to be a preferable source of truth.

How can one disprove an argument from an anecdote? Going back to the previous example, how would you disprove the claim that Newton's law predicts that planets will move in an ellipsis? Do you need to prove that they don't move in an ellipsis? That can't be done because planets do follow an elliptical curve. It is the conclusion "therefore Newton's law of gravity is correct" that doesn't necessarily follow from the claim, but that is also difficult to demonstrate. There is a possibility that the law is correct after all, in which case, the argument may be reasonable. It is only in the light of a different theory, such as relativity, that this argument from an anecdote becomes less convincing. Einstein's theory has the same potential to explain the facts that the argument was based on, but the good thing with these two theories was that we had measurements and we could differentiate one from the other, the correct from the incorrect. Without them, as is the case with the theory of evolution and its hypothetical competitor, the only thing we could possibly demonstrate is that both scenarios fit the same facts. We could not illustrate which is better, but we could show that both are equally viable, which means neither is definitely true. That is all we can do, and that is all I can do, and that is all I will do.

Finding an alternative theory by which all of the anecdotes of evolution could be potentially explained is both challenging and also straightforward at the same time. It is challenging because there aren't that many theories to choose from and also straightforward, for the exact same reason. Historically, the theory that preceded the theory of evolution was the idea of special creation, in which a God has created all organisms and, perhaps, more and, even today, this is the only non-Darwinian alternative to the theory. I don't have much choice in what I can compare evolution with, but I don't think this is a bad thing. As a matter of fact, I think creationism is the best choice available for one simple reason: nobody in the scientific community takes creationism seriously. Thus, if I can demonstrate that a hypothesis like creationism can just as easily explain the same facts as Darwin's theory, then nobody could argue that those hypotheses had any value to begin with. If they are so malleable that they could fit something like a myth from a religious book, then their value was greatly exaggerated or, perhaps, that myth had more truth to it than anyone dared to think.

As this is a highly controversial topic, two rules must be followed for the whole act of comparing to have any meaning. First, we must make the best argument for creation that we could possibly make and, second, we must do an objective comparison between the two theories. Seems simple, but I don't think anyone has ever succeeded with these tasks, which is either the reason for or the result of the controversy surrounding the idea of creationism. The idea of creation has a very long history, but in scientific circles, it fell out of favor after Darwin came to prominence. The most recent and most modern incarnation of the hypothesis is called Intelligent Design (ID), which has been widely recognized as a pseudo-scientific idea. While this may be true, it is, perhaps, the most rational variation of the idea of creation. According to ID, life and other phenomena of the universe are best explained by an intelligent designer, and this is what it seeks to prove; however, the theory itself doesn't seek to identify the designer himself. Regardless of the reason why they don't wish to identify this creator, not identifying it or him is a major issue for this theory. A proper scientific theory would at least attempt to figure out everything possible regarding this hypothetical entity. If an intelligent designer is the cause of anything and the theory seeks to prove that, then it is absolutely crucial to establish what that cause really is or is like. Since ID does not properly defines the designer in any shape or form, I will need to create my own theory of creation. For now, the only thing that is important about this theory is that it will be called the theory of natural creation because it will be a theory about creation based on natural phenomena exclusively. Thus, myths and texts of revealed religions will be omitted from evidence for obvious reasons. It will be based on nature and nature only, which doesn't mean it will be the truth, just that it will be based on established scientific facts.

The theory of natural creation seeks to explain how living organisms could have been created by intelligent causes. To do this, I will look at observable instances of intelligent causes in action and compare their products to those found in nature. Finding intelligent sources in the universe is not difficult, as humans are the only known source of this phenomenon.

Stones don't create complex instruments, and neither do monkeys, at least not to the extent humans can. If we wish to understand creation, then we need to observe how humans create, and because we wish to compare the result of these processes with other living beings, we should examine those human creations that produce similar results. As organisms are primarily defined by their genes and DNA, it makes sense to suppose that, if life was created, it was created by engineers who could code things like the genetic code. In our world, this would be software engineers or, in the very least, those in a profession similar to it. As luck would have it, my profession is quite similar to that of a software engineer, so I feel confident that I will be able to reveal the mysteries of this profession.

A philosopher might argue that it isn't correct to compare the hypothetical design process of organisms to human engineering because clearly humans could not be responsible for creation. Humans cannot be the cause of life, as they are living beings and could not be brought into being by their own volition, not to mention that life predates humans by billions of years. Given all of this, it's apparent that nobody would claim that humans are the creators of life on our planet, but that doesn't mean that they cannot be used as an example of architects to establish what it would have been like if life were created by an intelligent being. This thought experiment might seem unscientific, but the truth is that similar arguments have been quite common in certain fields of science. In archaeology, it is perfectly natural to infer that certain sculptors existed based on the statues they crafted, even if the people themselves or any record of their existence has been lost to the passage of time. For example, why is it that we could believe that people called the Olmecs existed in the past, based solely on the fact that several gigantic statues have been found in Central America? Nobody has ever seen an

Olmec or heard about one, but because we found a number of statues, archaeologists concluded that they must have been a civilization of humans simply because those statues were similar to the objects created by other civilizations, such as the Greeks. Of course, the Olmecs were not identical to the Greeks, they are just similar to them in that they both created statues of humans, though they appeared to differ in everything else, except being humans. An extraterrestrial intelligence predating DNA-based life forms would also be similar to the Greeks—and to modern humans in some respects—by being capable of creating complex tools, though it would be different in other ways, such as not being from the same planet. Suggesting that an intelligent being should not be considered a potential cause of life because they could not be humans is like suggesting that the Olmecs should not be considered to have existed because they were not Greeks. If finding an alien statue or a statue of an alien on the moon, or a specific radio signal coming from a star system could be treated as an example of extraterrestrial intelligence, then so can anything else. Ultimately, what should decide such questions is the evidence that we find and not any preconceived notion of what should or shouldn't exist in the universe.

The most commonly used arguments for the theory of evolution are those that fall into a category I call the arguments for common descent and the tree of life. The original idea of a tree was developed by Darwin, but his tree was quite simple, and his concept has been expanded greatly in the many decades that followed. The arguments include a set of facts, such as fossil and genetic evidence, but they all support the same idea that all organisms are related to each other, some more than others, and that their relationships can be put on a graph resembling a tree. For example, we can find different fossils in different layers of rocks, depending on

which geological era the organisms lived in, and similar fossils
of different species can be found on top of each other, which
strongly suggests change over time. Genetic evidence demonstrates that organisms from different species that are close to
each other morphologically tend to be close genetically as
well, which proves that their relationship goes beyond a similarity in appearance. Some of these related species are also
located in closer proximity to each other, though still separated by geographical barriers such as seas and deserts, which
supports the idea of a common ancestor. The arguments favor
common descent, which is a cornerstone of evolution, and the
facts I mentioned—similarity of fossils and genes and the
proximal geographical distribution of both—are indeed consistent with common descent and the principles connected to
the tree of life. Common descent explains why these natural
phenomena are what they are, but that's not the same as
proving the theory of evolution. The evidence is consistent
with evolution, but common descent is not the only theory it
might be consistent with.

The tree of life is a simple progressively expanding graph
that starts with a single common ancestor and then branches
out into several families of organisms, which, in turn, branch
out further. Every living being is connected to every other
being on this graph, and any two organisms have a single
common ancestor somewhere on the tree. The closer this
ancestor is to the two species, the more closely related they are
and, thus, the more likely they will have similar genes and
forms. This graph very much fits the concept of common
descent, but we must not forget that, even though evolution is
a gradual, continuous process, on the tree of life we can only
find the successful major organisms and not anything in
between. Gaps exist between every species, both in the fossil
record and in the genetic data we possess, and the tree of life

does not provide any evidence of gradual change. Thus, any alternative hypothesis would not need to provide such evidence either. The facts are that certain organisms have existed at certain places in time and space, and many of those were very similar to each other, and a distinct notion of progress can be derived when these organisms are looked at from afar. An alternative theory must only explain the facts and not the guesses that have been derived from the facts by the other theory.

Do graphs that look similar to common descent exist in software engineering, or is this something unique to life on Earth? The answer is, of course they exist. This is a common pattern in software development. It is true that not all software is developed in a way that, if we put different versions of the same software on a graph, it would resemble a tree-like shape, but there is a large chunk of programs that do. These are called open-source software and, by the very nature of the way they are developed, graphs delineating their development will place each iteration of the software in a way that will resemble the relationships found on the tree of life.

"Open-source" denotes a form of software development in which the source code of the software is accessible to anyone and, in many cases, can be copied and changed by anyone as well. Programmers cannot change the original code of others without their consent, but they can copy the code and change it for themselves and opt to send the changes back to the original developer. The open-source paradigm actively facilitates collaboration between engineers by giving access to the source code of software and not just the computer code, the latter being much less readable by human beings. One of the oldest and most widely used open-source software is the operating system called Linux. This operating system, or rather the distributions based on it, which are extended versions of the original system, can be found on a multitude of devices, from personal computers and mobile phones to servers and televisions. It is used everywhere. As it is open-source, everyone can copy it and make their own version of the software. On the desktop side, people can make their own distribution of Linux, which can then be copied and altered by others, and then those copies can be copied again, and so on. Some distributions will become popular and will be developed continuously for a long time, while others loose popularity and development stops for most of those. As the popular distributions are used by countless people, they are often used as a base for new distributions, which gives birth to multiple new versions of that operating system.

The tree of Linux, which is not an official term, looks very similar to the tree of life. In 2010, Andreas Lundqvist started gathering all desktop Linux distributions with their relationships to each other so that they could all be put on the same graph. He unintentionally created something that looked almost identical to the tree of life, at least visually. Every graph node on both the tree of life and the tree of Linux has only a single parent, but the same parent can have multiple child nodes. On both graphs, which also function as timelines, new child nodes appear all the time, but some nodes might also disappear because they either die out or because development stops, in the case of Linux. In the latter case, most are no longer used by anyone because they are simply too outdated for modern hardware, but their code still exists on the Internet or in someone's basement. These old operating systems are like the fossils of nature; they are the literal remnants of an older era that have mostly been forgotten. One important thing to note is that systems closer to each other tend to function, at least from a computing viewpoint, more similarly than those that are further apart, because the closer ones share more code. The same thing is true for living organisms on the tree of life: they, too, share more code and have a stronger resemblance of form the closer they are to each other.

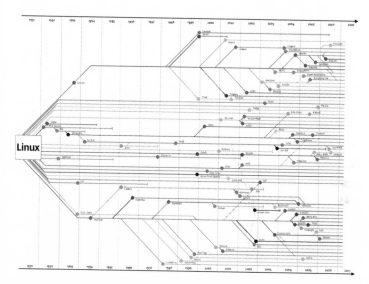

Tree of Linux

In addition, Lundqvist's graph had other features, such as a visual representation of patching between parallel branches. Sometimes the creators of one distribution want to grab source code changes from distributions that are closely related, as they believe that those changes would be beneficial for their distribution. Generally, they only take a small part of the other distribution's source code, and not everything. Essentially, they cherry-pick the part they want and simply copy it from the other codebase, attaining the equivalent of horizontal gene movement of genetics. As genes usually move from parent to child in real life, and vertically between species on the tree of life, they normally cannot pass from one parallel branch to another, except in cases of horizontal gene movement. Many instances of horizontal gene movement have been found between many different organisms. For example, one study found that 40 genes are found exclusivity in both humans and bacteria, but not in other vertebrates, implying that both bacteria and humans obtained the genes either from each other or from the same source via horizontal gene transfer, but because this interpretation of the evidence doesn't seem to be in favor of evolution *per se*, it is strongly disputed by academics. The prevalent accepted explanation is that those 40 genes have been in all of the progenitors of humans but got deleted by evolution over time from all other descendants. That is one interpretation of the evidence, and perhaps a far too convenient one for the theory of evolution, which disregards the concept of horizontal gene transfers for simply being annoying.

The genetic origins of humans seem to be quite complicated and not at all as simple as the tree of life would suggest. When the genetic relationship of humans, chimpanzees, and gorillas were analyzed, it was found that some genes are more similar between humans and chimpanzees than gorillas, some are more similar between humans and gorillas than chimpanzees, while still other genes are more similar between chimpanzees and gorillas than humans. How is this possible? How could you plot a graph of common ancestors for the tree of life, when everyone is related to everyone and no one at the same time? Well, there is a convoluted explanation for it, which I will not attempt to tell you, but there are ways to work around the problem of who had whose common ancestor and who didn't or shouldn't have. Suffice to say that the tree of life doesn't seem to be as clear cut as it was once believed, and it seems to be entangled the most where most of the research has been done. Perhaps, this is a mere coincidence, but, if not, a software architect would have a pretty simple explanation for the inconsistency between the tree of life and reality. We programmers do such cherry-picking all the time. If we like or need something, we put it in our code regardless of where it came from, as long as putting it there doesn't pose a threat in the form of fatal errors to the software or in the form of lawsuits to ourselves. In the case of open-source software, the latter is unlikely, which is why open-source has created an absolute mess of code dependence that, at this point in time, even computers have difficulty comprehending.

Not all software and not even all open-source software development iterations resemble the branching form of the tree of life. Linux being what most of the Internet runs on is a very exceptional piece of software and, as it has so many other applications, nobody truly knows how many different devices actually use it. The thing that all Linux-run machines have in common is their core, called the Linux kernel, which is a code-base that is being continuously written and updated by thousands of developers. Naturally, these coders may work on the same part of the kernel, which can easily lead to conflicts both in the code and in real life, if the former aren't resolved quickly. To solve this issue, Linus Torvalds, the creator and maintainer of the Linux kernel, has created the Global Information Tracker (GIT), a distributed version control system so that such conflicts may be managed and coders will not override each other's work or faces. GIT is the most popular solution to solve the issues of concurrent coding, but what should interest us the most is how this software relates to the concept of the tree of life. First, GIT has branches, or at least one, in which all our code sits. At any time, a new branch can be created from an existing branch and development can be done in parallel in these branches so that eventually they can be merged back together to form a single branch. Think of them as the breeds found in the animal kingdom, which are more like twigs on the tree of life, rather than branches. They are their separate entity, but they are still able to mix or be merged with the breed or branch they started from. In nature, different breeds often adapt to their own environments, which is also true for different branches of a GIT codebase. Typically, producing software requires at least a development, testing, and a production environment, each supplied with their corresponding branch so that different versions of the same code can be deployed to each environment. In GIT, we call a single codebase a repository, which is the hub of all related software branches and would be equal to the concept of a species in biology. Thus, if we wanted to upload the source code of dogs into GIT, "Dog" would be the name of our repository and "Labrador," "Husky," "Doberman," and all other breeds would be the branches of that repository. If we wanted to "make" a new breed or subspecies we could create a new branch from an existing one, but if we wanted to make a different species from a dog, a new solution would be required.

Creating branches are not meant to facilitate speciation or its software equivalent, but there are GIT functions that can do that. Any open-source GIT repository can be "forked" by anyone, that is, someone can make a referential duplicate of the whole repository with all of its branches intact. From that point onwards, the old repository and the new repository will be developed independently, although for a while it might be possible to still pull back the code from one into the other. A fork is the technical equivalent of a species from the graph of the tree of life, and because the distinction between a breed or subspecies and a species in nature is often not clear, these forks can be also sometimes mixed with each other, even in GIT, blurring the distinction between the two. For example, the Linux distributions called flavors, which are slightly modified versions of a popular Linux distribution, are far more similar to a breed than to a species. Linux, unlike other operating systems, has several graphics–user interfaces (GUI) and, because every distribution is packaged with one, developers who prefer a GUI different from the one in the main repository will often fork their distribution of choice and replace the GUI with their favorite. This is usually why a new flavor is created and, since a GUI can technically be replaced even after installing the operating system, a flavor is normally not treated as an independent distribution.

Furthermore, developers can also add their own code to the flavors or to another fork of a mainline distribution, making them more distinct and creating their own more-unique operating system. Eventually, the forked repositories might separate so much that mixing them directly becomes too difficult, even though the need to grab some code from one and put it into the other might still exist. In this case, the GIT action known as "cherry-picking" can be utilized to attain the desired result, which is, as mentioned earlier, equal to the horizontal gene movement that is rarely represented on the tree of life. If even that is impossible, a programmer can simply copy the text from one codebase and paste it into his own repository, which sometimes is the only solution when the two programs are as far apart as bacteria would be from humans.

The purpose of comparing the version control system GIT to the tree of life is to demonstrate that, thanks to the way GIT works, patterns like the tree of life will appear repeatedly during software development. As a matter of fact, it is simply impossible to produce something that doesn't resemble the structure of the tree of life in GIT. Given that about half of all software is open-source, and most of that is found in GIT repositories, the similarities between it and the tree should not be taken lightly. It is not a coincidence that some software is developed this way. In software engineering, practicality is king, and GIT is a very practical solution to the complex problem of multiple developers working on the same thing. This does not mean that if life was developed by a creator, he must have created organisms this way because he needed to collaborate with others, as there may be other legitimate reasons why a creator would have chosen this path. I will try to explain later why developing life this way might make sense from an engineering standpoint. For now, we should acknowledge that patterns like the tree of life are quite common in software development and so the existence of the pattern will not provide proof for any theory, be it evolution or creation.

Going one level below the subspecies of the phylogenetic tree, we find that one strange feature of living organisms compared with software is the fundamental variability of each specimen of a species. Such differences are relatively uncommon in programs, as the software code on one computer is equal to the same software on another. This is not true for most species, as many encompass a group of specimens that have been created from a mix of genes that not all possess. Thus, the source code of living beings is variable, while the code made by programmers is not. Variability is a valuable asset in nature, as a species has a higher chance of survival if it can adapt to different environments, but the same cannot be said about computer programs. Natural or other types of selection generally don't work on programs, but there are exceptions. One such exception is what we call A/B testing, during which two units of the same feature are developed so that one could be selected as preferable by the program's users. For example, imagine that the home page of a website is developed, and we wish to entice the visitors to register on the site. As we don't know what people prefer, we develop two home pages A and B, and randomly show A to half of the visitors and B to the other half. We then record how many people visiting A and B registered and compare the result to determine which home page to use. In A/B testing, people take the place of natural selection, and while such methods are rarely used in programming, they are nevertheless used when deemed necessary, and there's no reason to believe that an intelligent agent would not use it to make life more sustainable.

Another often mentioned proof of evolution is the existence of vestiges, found mainly, at least for now, in the animal kingdom. Vestigial organs of animals have lost either part of or all the functionally they once possessed. For example, the blind mole rat's eyes, which are completely covered in skin, is one such vestigial organ. The ancestor of the mole rat probably lived on the surface instead of beneath it and had more use for functioning eyes, but, once the animal started living underground, its eyes became unnecessary and somehow degraded to their current state. According to modern science, that "somehow" was evolution, and I would argue that such evolution would make sense to some degree. The *E. coli* experiment revealed that degradation to minimize resource usage was a robust evolutionary tool. It is entirely possible that this is what happened to the ancestor of the blind mole rat as well.

There may be many instances of vestigiality through natural degradation, but we must nevertheless still ask whether such occurrences can also be created by intelligent agents or not. After all, the existence of vestigial organs is much more of an argument against creation rather than for evolution. Thus, are there any vestiges in software engineering? Yes, of course, but we use a different name. "Legacy" is a technical term used to describe a piece of software that has, in part, lost some or sometimes all of its functionality because of the release of new versions of the same software. Legacy is a natural byproduct of software requirements changing over time. The creation of the original code that later became unwanted was desirable in the past, but owing to outside changes, it became less desirable and, thus, became a legacy. No matter how good programmers are, it is usually only a matter of time before some of the code they worked on will change to this undesirable state.

Let us look at a quick example of how and why legacy code and other legacy software components are created. Imagine that you, as a programmer, have written a code for a smartphone application (app) and for the server that communicates with it. Let's suppose that the app becomes really popular and certain services are used so often in the app that the servers can't handle them and they begin to fail. Therefore, the decision is made to break apart the services into smaller services so that the servers can handle them better. A new version of the app and a newer version of the server is created by the engineers and a plan is set into motion to release them to the live audience. So far so good, but here's the problem: you can update the server almost instantaneously with a push of a button, but you cannot do the same for the thousands of handheld devices the app resides on. Of course, eventually everyone will update to the new application, but that will take some time, and it would be a problem if the users couldn't use the app until they do. After all, if the new servers provide services in smaller chunks than the previous versions, then the old apps won't be able to communicate with them. Thus, there is a need either to keep some older servers running so that they can service the apps that have not been updated, or to keep the old functionality from the previous versions of the server and provide data for both the new and the old apps. In the former case, we would have created a legacy server by our actions and, in the latter example, we would have used legacy services to keep the legacy apps running.

Legacy code and legacy apps and servers, in general, do not get frequent updates while everything else around them does, which can result in some form of degradation, especially if the apps that still rely on their functionality are limited in number. In this regard, legacy is very similar to vestigiality. We should also remember that living organisms are very different from smartphone apps and the phenomena of legacy might affect the former much more than our pocket instruments. Sometimes legacy code loses so much functionality that it becomes dead code, which means that it will no longer be referenced by the rest of the codebase unless by accident. Such accidents have historically cost billions of dollars to the companies that overlooked the existence of these code fragments in their software. Dead code is highly similar to certain noncoding and nonfunctional fragments that can be found in the genome of living organisms. It might seem strange that a creator would make living beings with either legacy code or dead code in their DNA; however, if we look at software engineers, this legacy phenomenon is something that they must handle regularly and not necessarily because they are bad at their jobs. As a matter of fact, they had to handle it so much that they came up with their own word and technical definition for it that almost all of them now know and understand.

Another popular example of vestigiality is the human eye, which allegedly has certain defects an intelligent designer would supposedly never allow to exist in his creation. One of these defects is the blind spot of the eye, which is caused by the fact that the blood vessels that feed the eye's light-sensitive cells need a place to enter the eye itself. Some animals' eyes, such as the octopuses' can supply oxygen from the outside of the eye, supposedly making their eyes better than the humans'. Notwithstanding the fact that the metabolism of an animal living in the deep sea is very different from ours, we still have to acknowledge that the design philosophy behind an eye that can't see color, and one that can see color might be slightly different. Besides, we should consider the fact that the brain uses the image data of one eye to hide the blind spot of the other eye, making it completely unnoticeable. If we close one eye, the brain will simply guess what kind of color or pattern should be visible in the place of the blind spot and shows us that instead of nothing. If we consider these facts, then the idea that the eye was not designed might be much less convincing. Fixing a design flaw or inadequacy of the hardware using software via "monkey patching," which is an actual term, is quite common in the information industry. For example, the security vulnerabilities known as Meltdown and Spectre, which were found in modern computer processors in 2018, were fixed by patching the operating systems that ran on the vulnerable processors rather than by fixing the hardware.

Vestiges can be found in many places, including in some parts of our DNA. The human genome contains sections known as endogenous retroviruses (ERVs), which are the remnants of ancient infections by viruses that have copied their own genetic material into human or human ancestral DNA. When a cell gets infected, a mutation could deactivate the virus, which is why all the ERVs we possess are no longer active and won't produce more viruses and infect other cells. ERVs are the vestiges of viruses, or at least that is the currently accepted hypothesis for the gene sequences desig-nated to be ERVs. Most of the sequences were found by searching through the human genome for parts that resemble the base sequences of known viruses. As they are inactive and most cannot be activated, it is hard to say if all ERVs resulted from viral infections or only some. It has been estimated that around 5%–8% of the human genome is comprised of ERVs, which is a significant amount if we consider that protein-coding genes account for only 1.5% of the genome. Another remarkable fact of some ERVs is that they are shared among species, meaning that they must have been inherited from a common ancestor. The idea that related species share similar genes or other base sequences is not new, but because ERVs are generally nonfunctional, it would be hard to argue that some entity has purposefully put them into different organisms, as that would not make any sense. Even in the world of software engineering, such post addition of dead code is almost unprecedented and, even if it wasn't, it would only highlight the incompetence of the engineers who added them. Engineering alone cannot give a satisfactory answer to the question of why ERVs exist, but that doesn't mean that the question is fundamentally not answerable.

In the grand narrative of evolution, many stories have been crafted to explicate how and why different species evolved into other species. Continuing this tradition, we can write our own stories for our own benefit. After all, living beings aren't exactly like computer programs, and they have certain traits that are missing from modern software. Rather than asking why engineers do a certain thing, we could ask why they would do a certain thing given certain conditions. So, why and in what circumstances would an engineer be responsible for the creation of ERVs? First, let's assume, for the sake of argument, that this hypothetical engineer is operating at a point in time when both living organisms and retroviruses already exist on Earth. When an engineer is tasked with creating a new living organism, there are only two paths the engineer can take to finish the task: make a completely brand-new organism from the ground up or use existing organisms as a template for the new one. Most human engineers would choose the latter path because using the existing codebase is usually much more efficient than starting from scratch. Creating a new organism like that would not explain the existence of ERVs, as the template or source for an organism does not possess retroviruses and so the organism cannot pass them to the new species that is being crafted. There is, however, a third option; one that is almost completely unique to living organisms. Every living being has one attribute that unites them and differentiates them from human machinery. They can all replicate, which provides unique options to all who wish to use them as a basis to create new life.

What if the template used for the organism is not a blueprint for the organism, but rather the very organism itself? In that case, the genome of the organism living on Earth would be modified directly to create a new species, and if that organism had any retroviruses in its genome, then those would be passed on when the new species is born. This possibility would easily solve the mystery of the existence of ERVs, but then we would have to ask why would an engineer, be it human or not, choose this option? Using the reproductive capabilities of living organisms has certain advantages. One is that the necessary machinery to create a new species would be on Earth and wouldn't need to be created. This might not be a big problem for single-celled organisms, but if the goal is something bigger and more complex, then the flexibility existing organisms provide can be an ideal solution to the problem of not having a factory that can create life. After all, no such factory of life has been found, other than the organisms themselves; so, if they exist, they are either not on Earth or too well hidden. While in programming such methods of development are extremely rare, in medicine and molecular biology, they are much more common. Genetically modified organisms (GMOs) are created by altering the genome of a living being, generally by modifying the seed of a plant to enhance certain properties of the organism. GMOs are mostly used in agriculture, but advancements have been made in other fields as well. Considerable research has gone into altering the genome of simple and not-so-simple bacteria, and even altering the human genome has become feasible and is used to cure certain diseases. Most of these applications of gene editing, including gene therapy for humans, usually require viral vectors that can inject themselves into the target cell's nucleus and edit the DNA there. These vectors are called viral because they are made from viruses, some of which are exceptionally adept at breaking into a cell and injecting their own genetic information into the DNA found there.

Gene editing of existing organisms is how genetic engineers create new breeds and even new species, so is it possible that all life or most of it has been created that way? Humans create new species this way because it takes much less effort to create life from the existing organisms than from nothing, as organisms have self-replicating capabilities to begin with. Is it possible that a non-human creator could have used viral vectors to inject new genetic information into existing organisms to create a new species? If that is how most of life was created, then it's possible that that process has left some evidence in the form of ERVs, as ERVs are technically the remnants of such viral infections. As a matter of fact, 5%–8% of the human genome has been identified as being comprised of retroviruses, so the possibility does exist. Even if the identified ERVs in humans and other living beings were completely accidental, it wouldn't necessarily mean that these organisms were not created by altering the genomes of other organisms. Gene editing can add new nucleobases to an existing DNA strand, but it can also remove them when necessary. If the vectors were made so that they would remove the viral elements after they were injected and processed, then the evidence of the infection would be lost forever. This process is similar to the patching that software needs to go through during an update and, in that process, that patch is usually removed after the update to save disk space.

A software patch contains the difference in executable code of two versions of the same program and, by applying the patch to the earlier version, the software would upgrade to the next. Patches usually contain less code than the actual software; they only contain the changes that have been made since the previous version to conserve space. As the changes are often disconnected, every section of change has to know where it must be copied into the code of the software. Therefore, every change must be an instruction that defines what should be changed and where. This is something relatively simple to create via a programming language, but what about doing the same in the genome? Can this selective updating process be done in DNA via some genetic means? Such tools do, in fact, exist in the genome of living organisms. They are called transposable elements but were known simply as "jumping genes" some time ago. These transposable elements are small chunks of DNA that can move from one segment of DNA to a different one, so they can jump from gene to gene. By putting many transposable elements into a retrovirus, which itself is also categorized as a transposable element, we could essentially create a software patch that could modify the organism or its offspring drastically. It might be difficult to turn a dinosaur into a bird, but the change does not need to happen all at once. Even with regular software patching, there exists a common practice of applying a series of patches when the software is behind by several versions relative to the most up-to-date one. In the case of living organisms, this serial application of patches could be done, even with a single retrovirus, by limiting the number of transposable elements that can be active before the first offspring is born. Then, after each generation, more of the transposable elements could be added or activated until the desired organism is born at last. This way, the genetic differences between each offspring can be limited so that they remain viable descendants for their parents, thus the transition would be much more gradual, although not as gradual as it would be via an evolutionary process.

Needless to say, complex organisms would require a lot of patches or transposable elements to be created. If every gene or alteration to a gene was done by transposable patching, then both the original transposable element and the affected gene might be still located in our genome. In this case, a large chunk of our DNA would be made of transposable elements in the form of repeated DNA sequences. Currently, it is believed that half of the human genome is made of transposable elements, which are mostly no longer active, as one would expect if they were the result of a previous patching effort. Half of the human genome is a significant amount, and the fact that transposable elements are so prevalent in DNA is something that the theory of evolution never predicted. Conversely, this is something that should be expected if organisms were created by an engineer who used retroviruses to transfer the information needed to alter the characteristics of existing organisms to create new species. The existence of ERVs and transposable elements do not prove that life was designed, but they are consistent with the idea and, if nothing else, they show how the process could have been executed by using existing tools readily available from the genome of every organism in nature.

Every story we create has the ability to move our imagination, regardless of it being real or fictional. This is both a blessing and a curse, as we may create stories that are both fact and fiction and, many times, we will not be able to tell the difference between the two. This is one of those cases. The best we can do is realize when we are crafting stories instead of discovering the history of the world so that we can tread lightly when we hypothesize about the past and not pretend that we know something that we cannot possibly prove. Science is the best tool to separate fact from fiction, but if it is not applied correctly, the two become inseparable and the process will be more about who can tell the better story rather than who is the closest to the truth. To realize this, one must be vigilant and humble, which are virtues sorely lacking in modern humans, but we must not forget that we are supposed to stand on the shoulders of giants and not growl at their feet.

Chapter 9

A Universe from Nothing

I n the last chapter, I stated that any theory about a creator would have to identify, or at least describe as much as possible, the one who supposedly created life. Therefore, a theory of natural creation must seek to answer who or what the creator was; otherwise, the theory is meaningless. This is a difficult question, but not for the reasons one might think. It would be easy to suggest that life on Earth was created and modified by aliens, in other words, by extraterrestrial life forms existing someplace else in the universe. Most naturalists would be open to accepting or at least entertaining the idea that life was seeded by aliens; however, this idea has some serious flaws. It seems to contradict the very reason why anyone would even consider the possibility of artificial creation, namely, that natural processes, such as evolution by natural selection, are not able to create the complexity we see in nature. According to the way complexity is measured in an ever-changing world, every object is as complex as the process that created it, and a simple process such as evolution is unlikely to have produced the complex organisms that are alive today. If we accept this premise to be true, then the creator of life would have had to be more complex than life itself, and if evolution is a lousy explanation for life's existence because of the gap in complexity, then it would not make sense to believe that the creator could have come about by evolutionary means. This creates a predicament that could easily question the validity of natural creation because if organic life was created by an intelligent being of the universe, then that alien would have to be eternal so that it would not need to be created by evolution. Such an eternal creator might have made sense a hundred years ago, but in a universe that was created in the Big Bang, eternity has almost completely lost its meaning. Aliens cannot be eternal because the universe is not eternal, so an explanation based on extraterrestrial influence can never adequately solve the question of life. If aliens cannot be the true cause of life, then what can be? Even if there is such a creator unlike any alien, would there be a single scientist willing to consider an option more extreme than aliens? Perhaps not, but I will consider it nonetheless, knowing that such explanations will not make anyone, including myself, too happy.

If we need to consider radical solutions to any question in science, we may only do so if there's a very good reason why we must go that far, even if the whole exercise is only a simple thought experiment. Being skeptical of evolution may not be a sufficient reason to speculate about the foundations of reality; after all, just because evolution doesn't work the way we thought it did, doesn't necessarily mean that there isn't an alternative to the process of evolution that is within the bounds of our current beliefs. Wouldn't searching for such an alternative be more reasonable than trying to force the idea of creation, despite its numerous issues? There's always a possibility that we have overlooked something or made some mistakes that we might realize later on. This being the case, we must have a good reason to go so far in our theorizing that we are willing to break scientific conventions in our quest to seek answers. The problems of evolution alone are not sufficient to justify such actions, but the theory of evolution has also led to some questionable answers and counterproductive views. As long as someone consistently accepts the implications of evolution, one will undoubtedly reach a few unconventional conclusions regarding the nature of the universe. One way or the other, the consequences of contentious ideas cannot be escaped as long as our ideas remain consistent with either evolution or creation.

The theory of evolution has instilled in naturalists the idea that from simplicity, complexity is born, either accidentally or inevitably, but always from a natural cause. Measuring complexity using algorithmic complexity makes it impossible for anything to be more complex than its source, but that doesn't mean that the complexity of a system cannot increase over time. It just means that there are limits to any system, and that complexity cannot be increased indefinitely because the system itself will not allow such a thing to happen. Unfortunately, the existence of these limits is not widely accepted in the scientific community, which has allowed the spread of the idea that from simplicity, complexity comes. After all, algorithmic complexity is just one way to measure complexity and if it is ignored, or not even taken into account, then there's no limit to the complexity that can be created, other than the imagination of people trying to measure it. Complexity is an attribute that is notoriously difficult to measure and so most won't even consider the change in complexity over time when coming up with a new hypothesis. Or even worse, many think that complexity can increase indefinitely from literal nonexistence, as if the information could be created from nothingness without any limiting factor. The laws of nature put limits on time, space, and energy, but not on information; however, that shouldn't mean that we consider its availability infinite, especially if we consider that everything else in existence has been determined to be finite.

Seeking simple answers to difficult questions has been the number-one goal of science for a long time. A simple or elegant answer has always been preferred to a complex or cumbersome answer because the former is easier to test or verify while the latter can rarely be checked with such ease, or perhaps not at all. The fact that the laws science has developed are both accurate and straightforward to an extreme degree has also helped further the idea that simple answers should be sought in the study of nature. Over the centuries, scientists have also discovered that some forces of nature were not, in fact, distinct from one another and could be unified into a single force. This is how the forces known as magnetism and electricity were unified into the modern concept of electromagnetic force. While not all new theories have been simpler than their predecessors, the trend has always been toward less complexity, unless a paradigm shift was occurring in science. A similar trend could be observed in cosmology. Originally, the universe was believed to be a constant existence with no beginning, but the Big Bang has clearly disproven that theory. Now, it is believed that all of the universe, including all the stars and all the galaxies, were born from a speck smaller than a ring on a person's finger. The universe didn't simply begin to exist, but rather started from an infinitely small existence relative to its current extent and has expanded and evolved into what we see now when we look up at the night sky. So, the universe was much, much simpler in the past, without stars or planets or even atoms, and only created those things later, as it became much more complex over time. Even here, the theme of "from simplicity comes complexity" can be easily discerned, just as in the story of biological evolution, so no wonder so few people are interested in where the complexity of the universe originated from.

Generally, scientists don't propose ideas that would break the limits of the boundaries of complexity in the universe. After all, whatever rule there is to limit the universe would undoubtedly limit the laws crafted to describe its true nature; therefore, the bounds of complexity for the universe must be respected, even if not directly. So, all is good, except for in a few cases where the new ideas have gone a bit far off from the laws and, consequently, from their limits. In such cases, the idea that from simplicity comes complexity has been taken to a ridiculous extreme, but why shouldn't that be normal? Doesn't evolution and the history of the universe strongly imply that simple things, simple laws, and simple particles are the origin of everything? So, wouldn't it be normal to follow the history of everything back to literal nonexistence, even if such an idea wouldn't normally make any sense? After all, how is it that all this complexity has been born from almost nothing, but a little bit of something cannot be born from literal nothingness? Really, what is the difference between the two? Complexity and information that did not previously exist got created as star systems and galaxies were formed, so why should we treat one idea as normal and the other as an impossibility? Wouldn't it make more sense to suggest that if so much came from almost nothing, then a little something can come into being from nothingness? You could even say that the scientists with these radical ideas are the ones who are following the trend and doing the right thing, while everyone else is left behind because of their attachment to their old and outdated ideas. If, on the other hand, the limits proposed in this book on complexity are more than mere convention and have been weaved into the fabric of reality from the beginning, then those who try to deny its existence aren't merely unconventional in their pursuit but have been completely wrong about the nature of the universe and the way they sought to uncover its secrets.

In any process, be it artificial or natural, complexity can increase as information is being transferred to the objects that take part in the process, but the nature of the process itself will always limit the amount of information gained by them. The more complex the process, the more information it can transfer to its products, but never more than the algorithmic equivalent of its own self. Denying this fundamental truth is deceit, the deceit of simplicity, and while not many scientists have subscribed to this philosophical falsehood, a few very influential theoreticians have done so to a large degree. In a way, this is a sensible decision to make, as not subscribing would inadvertently lead to questioning the tenets of evolution, which may be more damning for a naturalist. I will present a few examples of these questionable views promoted by scientists regarding the nature of the universe and the universe of living organisms, which seem to strongly correlate with the deceit of simplicity. We must, however, remember that these ideas are controversial by nature and by no means represent the consensus of science.

Almost all scientists have very sensible ideas regarding the nature of the universe, but a few notable researchers have shifted away from the mainstream and have started working on theories previously thought to be outside of the realm of science. One such theory can be found in Lawrence M. Krauss' 2012 book *A Universe from Nothing*, which suggests that the universe can and has come from nothing. Krauss bases his theory primarily on quantum mechanics, which allows for the spontaneous creation of particles in space, and suggests that such particles could have initiated the Big Bang that created our universe. He writes, "In quantum gravity, universes can, and indeed always will, spontaneously appear from nothing. Such universes need not be empty, but can have matter and radiation in them, as long as the total energy, including the negative energy associated with gravity, is zero."

The problem with such a theory is that the type of space in which particles can appear spontaneously differs from the type of space where that can't happen regardless if the particles appear in space or appear without any spatial property to speak of. Nothingness is the concept of what we would get if we would remove all properties from an object, including those we could only define with reference to potentiality. Whatever remains would be nothingness; an object without any property. That is, for lack of a better verb, what nothing is, and there are no other concepts that could be also called nothing in the context of metaphysics. If the universe came to be because of some event describable by quantum mechanics, then it did not come from nothing, at least not when nothing is strictly defined as something without properties or potentiality. Kraus argues that potentiality doesn't equal existence, and he uses the example that the capacity to have sexual intercourse with a woman won't necessarily result in a pregnancy, that is, in existence. He is right that potentiality is not destiny, but that doesn't mean that potentiality is not a property by which we can differentiate between any two objects. Whatever sexual potentiality one may have, it is probably not shared with a bacterium or a rock and, just because a glass has not yet been broken, it doesn't mean that it doesn't have the property of being brittle. The idea that the universe came from nothing is both unnecessary and wrong and seems to stem from the desire to make the beginning of the universe simpler than it actually was.

Krauss was not the only scientist who came up with or

supported the idea of a universe that came to be from nothingness. The late Stephen Hawking and Leonard Mlodinow have also suggested this idea in their book *The Grand Design* with a somewhat different argument, even though their conclusion was the same and it carried the same metaphysical issues as Krauss's argument. The book stated, "Because there is a law like gravity, the universe can and will create itself from nothing in the manner described in Chapter 6. Spontaneous creation is the reason there is something rather than nothing, why the universe exists, why we exist."

It is important to note that all three authors argued that, as the universe could and probably did come from nothing, there was no need to invoke God to create the universe. While this is technically true, they did not explain how a different universe, one that did not come from nothing, would change anything regarding the question of God's existence. Are we to believe that if the universe came from something that would prove that God exists? Surely that is not what they believe, but then why would they emphasize this point? If something other than God has created the universe, then that something would be the reason why the Big Bang happened and, whether this something is nothing or not nothing, doesn't really change anything. The only thing invoking nothingness as the source of creation does is that it weakens the argument and shifts the attention away from science to the philosophical issues that should not be there to begin with.

While *The Grand Design* mainly focused on the universe and its beginning, it also made some thought-provoking claims regarding living organisms and their origin. For example, Hawking and Mlodinow used John Conway's game of life algorithm to convey the idea that simple rules can produce complex entities. The game of life is a two-dimensional grid where every point is either empty or occupied by an organism.

As the game progresses, the digital organism either dies or reproduces based on how many or how few grid points are occupied next to them. Depending on the initial setup, the population of digital organisms generally either dies out, reproduces, and stagnates, or goes into some sort of looping sequence. Hawking and Mlodinow go so far as to suggest that not only life but even intelligent and self-conscious life, can simply arise from a set of simple rules. They write, "The example of Conway's *Game of Life* shows that even a very simple set of laws can produce complex features similar to those of intelligent life." They suggest that any entity that is so complex that its actions cannot be predicted should be treated as an object with free will and, therefore, one that is intelligent. Even if we accept this premise, how Conway's game has or can create such an entity is not entirely clear. You can always calculate the next step of the game from the current generation and, even if that is not possible, you can just run the game to see what happens. Just because we cannot see an unspecific number of steps into the future doesn't mean we cannot predict what will happen. Just use a computer, and it will tell you the outcome. Regardless of whether intelligent life can be defined with reference to unpredictability, we should realize that these claims of life and intelligent life coming into existence from simple rules have not been substantiated with relevant evidence. If I am wrong and such evidence exists, then I would like to meet some intelligent beings created by Conway's game and have a conversation with them to confirm that they are intelligent and that I was wrong. At the very least, they should be able to do an IQ test and get an average score of 100 or pass a Turing test.

As the previous examples have shown, being a scientist will not discourage someone from accepting the idea of simple rules creating complex things, but one might wonder if the same is true for engineers as well? Would someone whose work is to solve complex problems by creating equally complex solutions have the same attitude toward this idea? I do not know, but based on my experience, my guess would be that an engineer would find it more difficult to accept such a proposition. After all, if the job of an engineer could be replaced by a simple algorithm like evolution, then one wouldn't find it strange that an engineer would disagree with the statement, notwithstanding it is true or not. For now, software engineers, not computers, write software, but if the process of evolution had the creative power it has been credited for, then there's no reason to believe that it could not easily replace the work of programmers. After all, based on the theory of evolution, no legitimate reason explains why we could not solve a complex problem by writing an evolutionary algorithm and running it on a supercomputer. It is almost always easier to write an evolutionary algorithm than a well-thought-out program to solve a specific problem, and yet few engineers would use this method to solve a problem, despite the almost unlimited computational power available in the present. Certainly, we don't have the millions of years that nature does to finish a single piece of software, but would we really need that much time with our current capacity to compute? If it took nature a few hundred million years to create the human brain, can't we create far simpler software in much less time using an evolutionary algorithm and modern computers? Software projects take months or even years to complete, so if we can generate the same software in the same time frame but with much fewer human resources, then we could make a lot of profit by doing so.

According to the theory of evolution, it doesn't matter at all how simple an evolutionary algorithm is; what matters is the environment and the pressure it puts on organisms. So, if we can set up the right environment in a digital space, we should be able to evolve any kind of program. This is a difficult task, but not at all impossible for a programmer to achieve. In software engineering, we have the concept of automated tests, which are short programs that test the software by running it with predefined parameters to see if it will give the correct results. If all tests pass, we view our program as one that solves the problem. Some programmers go as far to not write a single line of code before they have created all of their tests, which is commonly referred to as test-driven development (TDD). These tests are usually much easier to create than the program they are instructed to test and, by writing them in advance, we can create the evolutionary environment that can filter the good programs from the bad. Naturally, generating a program that can pass several thousand tests at the same time is pretty much impossible, but what if we generate a program that is only required to pass the first test? That should be easy, no? And if we have it, we can change our environment so that only a program that passes the first two tests instead of just the first will be acceptable, and we mutate our existing algorithm until it gets accepted. We continue this process, adding tests one at a time until all tests pass and, if done right, we will have a complete program at the end without having to write a single line of code. If evolution is a perfectly viable method to solve complex problems, then there's no reason to believe that we couldn't generate the software from the tests of the software, and yet programmers won't even attempt to do this, even though in theory it is far easier to write tests than good code. What this means is that programmers and their work are both meaningless and unnecessary, as they can be easily replaced by evolutionary algorithms and a few people writing tests. This is one of those unwanted consequences that the theory does not state clearly but strongly implies, and few realize what this really means. It has been often claimed by those opponents of evolution who subscribe to a certain belief system that if evolution is true, then human life has no value. Well as it turns out, it's only my life as a software engineer that doesn't have any value, according to the theory of evolution.

The implicit consequences of the theory of evolution affect the worldview of both engineers and scientists, but it does not affect them the same way. Most people in these two groups rarely need to interact with each other, so very few need to deal with the consequences directly, but some are not so lucky and have no choice in the matter. One such person is Stephen Wolfram, who is both a software engineer and a scientist. As someone who has done work in both fields, he has no choice but to deal with the repercussions of Darwin's theory, and it has been interesting to see how he tries to mitigate the dilemma created by evolution. In his 2002 book, *A New Kind of Science,* he addresses the issues of evolution, but his conclusions might astonish you, as his arguments seem to suffer from the worst case of the fallacy of simplicity you can imagine. Whether his arguments came from a misguided trust in the theory of evolution is difficult to ascertain, but it is probably true that evolution is at least partially to blame for the existence of his unconventional ideas. I would argue that the whole premise of his book has been guided by a false belief in simple algorithms being the source of complexity and that this was the cause of the book's poor reception and why, ever since its release, Wolfram's wish for a new kind of science has not been fulfilled. In the book, Wolfram writes the following on the prospects of evolution:

> The problem of maximizing fitness is essentially the same
> as the problem of satisfying constraints that we discussed at

the end of Chapter 7. And what we found there is that for sufficiently simple constraints – particularly continuous ones – iterative random searches converge fairly quickly to an optimal solution. But as soon as the constraints are more complicated this is no longer the case. And indeed, even when the optimal solution is comparatively simple it can require an astronomically large number of steps to get even anywhere close to it.

So far, so good. This is what you would expect from Wolfram the software engineer, but later he suggests that:

On the basis of traditional biological thinking one would tend to assume that whatever complexity one saw must in the end be carefully crafted to satisfy some elaborate set of constraints. But what I believe instead is that the vast majority of the complexity we see in biological systems actually has its origin in the purely abstract fact that among randomly chosen programs many give rise to complex behavior.

So rather than doubting evolution, as a scientist, he chooses to simply conclude that biological organisms aren't that complex because, according to him, many simple programs create complex behavior. As an example, he points to the cellular automata described in his book and proposes that those, too, are very simple programs that create complex behavior and, therefore, life may be similar in that regard. Wolfram's cellular automata do look indeterministic, but the only use people have found for them were as pseudo-random generators, and that does not prove that they are of equal complexity as, for example, the eyes and brains of any animal. Wolfram calls his idea the Principle of Computational Equivalence, which supposes that programs above a certain threshold are equally sophisticated and that this is why complex organisms can be created by simple processes. Essentially, he turns complexity from a quantity to quality, just as Hawking and Mlodinow suggested in their book, which implies that single-celled organisms and humans are equally complex, that the same amount of information is required for a human to survive as is necessary for a cell to survive, and that this is just how the universe works. Whether one is willing to accept these preconceptions as true does not change the fact that these are very radical ideas.

The questions of biological life only take up a minuscule part of *A New Kind of Science*. Most of the book deals with the idea of how science could be superseded by searching for simple algorithms in a virtual space of infinite algorithms. How one might find new laws by simply creating numerous algorithms and picking out those that generate the results that match nature and experience is not exactly clear. This way of finding new laws has not been very fruitful, and why would we expect it to be? Finding new laws by searching the virtual space of all algorithms might be a novel idea, but it is also one that does not make much sense, unless it is really easy to find algorithms that can solve real problems. Certainly, the idea of evolution seems to have no issue with this proposition, but reality might have a different opinion on this matter. Reality does not care what we hope to be true. There is not a human being alive today who could not be fooled by an illusion of complexity, but the same cannot be said about our computers, and the fact that our machines have not been providing us with the results we desire is not their fault, but ours. It doesn't matter how brilliant an individual is if his premises are flawed; the conclusions he will reach will be just as flawed, and no amount of hard work will or can change that. Wolfram's decision to treat all programs capable of computation equally has led his research astray and, as long as he continues down this path, he will probably never find any meaningful answers to the questions he sought.

Being a scientist will not make one believe in these radical ideas, but being a scientist and trying to construct a worldview that is consistent with the theory of evolution can have serious consequences for the way one tries to understand our reality. As long as someone doesn't take evolution into account when constructing their worldview, everything should be fine, but once they do that, things may break apart or must be broken to support this new worldview. Things that were complex must become simple, and things that were simple must become even simpler, to the point that they might become as simple as nothingness itself. From nothing, nothing comes, but to create more information from less, it would be really convenient if everything came from nothing, because if we accepted that premise, from that point on, it would become the rule rather than the exemption. Consequently, the problem of complexity would become a trivial issue.

If we look around our universe, we can observe that simple rules cause simple effects. The four fundamental forces expressed in the laws of nature and the few elementary particles with their handful of properties have created a large, but very simple universe. Owing to the random effects of the laws of quantum mechanics, the universe has become very diverse, but diversity does not equal complexity. Just as nothing cannot create anything but nothing, so can random-ness only create more randomness and noise, which obscures information rather than creates it. The location and arrange-ment of star systems are strongly influenced by the random effects of quantum mechanics, but the reason why such systems form in our universe to begin with is because of the nonrandom properties of the laws of nature. Patterns such as the arrangement of our solar system could not be the result of random effects, as randomness by its very definition lacks any possibility of creating a system based on a pattern. Therefore, we see this universe around us, with simple laws organizing fundamental particles into simple objects and creating systems that can be predicted billions of years in advance. All objects in nature, or at least all that we can discover, seem to follow the simple program of the universe, all but one: Earth. The moon, the planets, our sun, and anything we can detect with our instruments are made of randomly arranged and simple parts following a predetermined course, but not Earth at least, not anything that is on the surface of our little blue planet.

One could argue that because we can observe only a fraction of the universe, we should not expect to find the kind of complexity that exists on Earth in the form of organisms on other planets of our solar system, especially if life is supposed to be a sporadic occurrence in the universe. While this argument may seem to make sense, we must remember that just because we cannot see every part of the universe doesn't mean that there are complex objects somewhere else in the universe. Furthermore, we may not need to observe them to infer their existence from an intermediate cause. For example, if we could detect certain types of radio waves coming from the inaccessible parts of the universe, we could possibly infer the existence of complex intelligent beings as their source. The telescopes of the SETI project have been seeking such radio waves, but as of yet, haven't found any that were of extraterrestrial origin. If aliens did exist and if some of them were intelligent, then we could expect them to use radio waves for the same reason we use them ourselves. In 2018, the physicist Michio Kaku predicted, "I personally feel that within this century, we will make contact with an alien civilization, by listening in on their radio communications." At present, we have not yet found any alien radio signals, despite discovering many exoplanets that could theoretically support intelligent life.

The fact that we have not been able to find any evidence of intelligent beings in a different part of the galaxy, coupled with the fact that we haven't found any complex entities in our solar system, except on Earth, does not mean that no such things exist elsewhere in the universe. It does mean, however, that such claims are not supported by evidence and are generally very speculative. Even Michio Kaku agrees with this point. If life began naturally, we have no idea what the likelihood of another event like that to occur is because we can't reproduce the process that created life, despite all our knowledge and efforts to produce life. We must not forget that the laws that allow the existence of complex organisms are not necessarily the same as those that would create them naturally, unless we claim to have perfect knowledge of all of creation and know for a fact that the laws we found are the only laws that exist and therefore nothing else could be responsible. One should not assume that the universe is brimming with life simply because life exists on Earth, as there can be no valid reason to have that belief at this moment. Most of our solar system is barren and not very complex, and the only exception is a complete mystery, which should not be used as an example of a rule that assumes that life will create itself as long as some unknown condition is met. The more reasonable rule to assume would be that the universe was organized by simple laws that created a simple universe. Therefore, any part that we cannot observe is probably just as simple as the things we can observe, and the existence of life on Earth is simply a mystery that we cannot explain with our current knowledge. To suggest that something is out there that we have no evidence of would only be a pretense of knowledge and not real science.

Regarding the big questions of the universe, I believe that our approach should be that of the late Richard D. Feynman who in a 1981 BBC interview said:

> the way I think of what we're doing is we're exploring, we're trying to find out as much as we can about the world. People say to me, "Are you looking for the ultimate laws of physics?" No, I'm not, I'm just looking to find out more about the world and if it turns out there is a simple ultimate law which explains everything, so be it. That would be very nice to discover. If it turns out it's like an onion with millions of layers and we're just sick and tired of looking at the layers, then that's the way it is, but whatever way it comes out its nature is there and she's going to come out the way she is, and therefore when we go to investigate it we shouldn't predecide what it is we're trying to do except to try to find out more about it. If you say your problem is, why do you find out more about it, if you thought you were trying to find out more about it because you're going to get an answer to some deep philosophical question, you may be wrong. It may be that you can't get an answer to that particular question by finding out more about the character of nature, but I don't look at it [like that]. My interest in science is to simply find out about the world, and the more I find out the better it is, like, to find out.

Feynman doesn't put any arbitrary limits on nature, and he doesn't believe that he needs to do anything else but find out more about the world. A bit later in the interview, Feynman continues:

You see, one thing is, I can live with doubt, and uncertainty, and not knowing. I think it's much more interesting to live not knowing than to have answers which might be wrong. I have approximate answers and possible beliefs and different degrees of certainty about different things. But I'm not absolutely sure of anything, and there are many things I don't know anything about, such as whether it means anything to ask why we're here, and what the question might mean. I might think about it a little bit; if I can't figure it out, then I go onto something else. But I don't have to know an answer. I don't feel frightened by not knowing things, by being lost in the mysterious universe without having any purpose, which is the way it really is, as far as I can tell — possibly. It doesn't frighten me.

His words are worth remembering; if not forever, at least for the next chapter.

Chapter 10

A God from Something

In the previous chapter, we discussed how severely the untold implications of the theory of evolution can affect someone's worldview and how even the fundamentals of metaphysics and information theory would have to be redefined to accommodate all of them. This chapter will show that people who deny evolution have a similar problem and that there are no simple solutions to the questions Darwin sought to answer. As long as we are adamant about taking sides, we will no doubt reach a place that is not very desirable for us to be in. We must always remember that we always have the option to suspend judgment and wait for more evidence or better arguments to pop up. If we accept the words of evolutionary biologists or deniers as gospel, then neither group will have to improve their arguments because both would "take security in the false refuge of consensus" in their respective bubbles. We can be, and perhaps should be, agnostic regarding the question of the origin of life because who could be more impartial than someone who simply claims to not know the answer to the question? There have been far too many scholars who claimed to know the answer to the mystery of mysteries based solely on the arguments made by people in the past who had known far less about life than we do now, and we certainly don't need any more of that. It would be much nicer to see people without vested interests take up the mantle for a change and try to achieve progress without conforming to any group's desired outcome or world-view. Rather than working on evolutionary biology exclusively or inventing creation biology yet again, we should create a new field of science that we could call origin biology. Even as a thought experiment, we could try to look at the facts as we see them before us and not try to shove them into a preconceived system of expectations. In this manner, we can construct a new solution that we have yet to consider. If our goal is to understand the world more deeply, then going back to the basics should not be viewed as a threat, but rather as an absolute necessity. It is only by reconstructing the theory from the ground up that we can hope to ensure that the science stays healthy and does not fall into a pit from which there is no return. We should always remember that compromise in scientific thought is like a virus; it will not only destroy the ones who have it, but affect the other fields as well, because if it can spread, it will.

Starting over from scratch would be a very difficult task to accomplish, which is why I have no desire to even attempt such a thing. My part in this endeavor will be to critique Darwin's theory and that alone, as I am not qualified or wish to accomplish anything more than that. To do this, however, we must understand how the creator from our earlier hypothesis could fit into scientific thought and the universe itself. That said, we must remember that the point of the theory of natural creation was to show how an alternative hypothesis could be competitive and be even better than the theory of evolution, and not to argue that it is, in fact, a good theory.

The reason why we need it, other than the fact that we have no alternatives, is to demonstrate how weak the theory of evolution really is and not to provide a faulty answer to a question we have no answers for. The problem with the theory of natural creation, or any kind of creationist theory for that matter, is that it is really challenging to find a creator that can fit into our universe. The only creators we know of are us and, while we can use humans as an example for any kind of hypothetical maker, to identify such a being, we must look outside the boundaries of our solar system. Unfortunately, the laws of nature are not complex enough to bring into existence a complex being such as a human, or even a single-celled organism; thus, finding a creator even within the boundaries of our universe should be impossible. The fundamental simplicity of our universe was the premise we worked with until now, and we cannot throw it away at the moment it becomes inconvenient for our theory. For those of us like myself who have never been part of any religion, it would be much easier to accept an answer that involves extraterrestrial aliens as the potential creators of life but, unfortunately, that option is not available, and that is why the creationist viewpoint will never be digestible for most modern-day naturalists.

Our creator cannot be bound by the known laws of nature because the laws collectively expressed in the form of the algorithm of the universe are too simple to have been able to create the complex entities we call life. This is quite the predicament because science is normally unable to cope with anything that is supposed to be beyond the limits of nature. Nature is generally defined as everything that exists, and so anything that is not within nature literally does not exist. This is a metaphysical problem and, therefore, warrants a metaphysical answer. We do not need to demonstrate that things outside nature do, in fact, exist; only that the existence of such things in the proper context is philosophically sound. The question here is how certain we can be regarding the extent of the universe and the laws that govern it. We can only observe the things we can observe, and if there's something beyond that, we would not be able to tell unless there was a way to infer the existence of whatever we cannot detect. This issue normally crops up in regard to past events, so it is usually caused by the passage of time. For example, the Big Bang was an event in the past that we will never ever be able to observe, and we can only infer that it happened indirectly from the remnants of the event and nothing else. This fact does not make the proposition less scientific; quite the contrary. In this case, it shows how certain physicists are that the event really happened because otherwise, they would never dare to make such a proposition. The question of the creator is similar in that whatever the creator has done, we can only observe indirectly; however, in the creator's case, it isn't simply displaced in time like the Big Bang is, but in space as well. The question here is whether a space outside the universe could potentially exist, with different laws and occupied by an unknown creator, and whether such a proposition would be scientific.

Think about it this way. Ever since science has started its journey, our understanding of the universe evolved over time as we acquired new knowledge. There was a time when we believed that the Earth and the objects we could see in the sky were the only things that existed. Then there was a time, after we started making telescopes, when we believed that every star in the night sky was as large as our sun and that our sun was gigantic. And then, we realized that some of the stars we could see through our telescopes were not stars, but galaxies, which were just as large or even larger as our Milky Way. So, over the centuries, our conception of the universe shifted from our solar system to one galaxy and then to many galaxies.

Today, we have even gone further than that by estimating the mass of the universe without being able to observe all of what's out there. The important thing to note here is that, since the inception of science, and even before that, we had some understanding of where the limits of our universe were and, almost every time we thought that we were right, we turned out to be wrong. As our knowledge expanded, the universe has also expanded, and so it makes no sense to put any arbitrary limit on existence itself. It may be that everything began in the Big Bang and all of it is governed by the laws of nature, but it's also possible that nature is larger than that and we have yet to see its full extent. As Richard Feynman put it, the universe might be like an onion, and we might be just in the center with countless slices above us. If that is the case, then the creator would probably be located on the slice directly above us. And because "above" means "super" in Latin, we could call this the supernature, which is directly above the nature that we reside in. Accordingly, nature cannot simply mean everything that exists, but rather the universe or the collection of things that came to be in the Big Bang and are governed by the known laws of nature. Philosophically, supernature is similar to the proposition of the multiverse, which is also not governed by our laws and did not began in the Big Bang, but similar only in its fundamental metaphysics. Whether there's evidence to support either of these ideas is an entirely different question though.

Until now, when we discussed a creator, we didn't necessarily mean an intelligent being but rather a cause that was more complex than our universe and was responsible for the creation of life. Only when we introduce the possibility of an intelligent cause can we add this attribute to our hypothetical creator. The justification for doing this would be that we have determined that life is remarkably similar to the objects we humans have designed over the years, and, therefore, there is a possibility that life was designed by an intelligent being as well. The latter conclusion does not require the creator to be supernatural, but the argument from complexity does because it does not allow any creator to exist in the same universe as life itself. Based on the argument from design and the argument from complexity, we can postulate that the creator of life must be both supernatural and intelligent, which are attributes generally associated with God. If a creationist would need to invoke the same idea, they would probably use the term intelligent designer to avoid prejudice, but because I am a third-generation nonbeliever, it would not make much sense to censor myself the same way. This is also why I am not afraid to use terms like "supernature" and "supernatural," as the only concepts I mean by those words are the things that I have already described and nothing more. Of course, this also means that, when I use the term "god," I also only mean what I have already stated and nothing more. I certainly don't believe that this god should be associated with the God of Christianity or any other religion; however, the possibility is technically still there, as long as the connection can be proven by scientific means. I personally am not aware of any legitimate argument that could possibly achieve such a feat, so, at the moment, there's no point in entertaining this possibility or, at the very least, not by me.

The critical question we must ask is whether God as a concept can in any way be part of a legitimate scientific theory or rather, in what way, can he be part of one. In the mainstream of scientific thought, it has been prevalent to think of God as something that science has nothing to say about, either because it doesn't exist, cannot exist, or because only religion can say anything meaningful about God. This view is commonly referred to as methodological naturalism, which has been very popular for a while in certain secular circles despite the fact that it was originally invented by theists. This term was designed to separate science from religion to protect religion from science, as well as science from religion. It is fundamentally a theological worldview because it presupposes that there are things such as God that exist, which science can say nothing about, even though science is the study of nature, that is, the study of things that exist. Why any secular scientist would promote such an idea is a bit of a mystery, but I blame it on a general disdain and lack of interest in the study of philosophy on the scientist's part. The important thing, though, is that if God exists, we can only infer that through science and the question itself should be completely within the realm of scientific thought. The problem, of course, comes when we want to understand how we can infer the existence of a supernatural entity when it is fundamentally impossible to detect such beings currently through direct or indirect observation. When we see something in nature, we normally try to explain the existence of that something as a consequence of some natural process set in motion by a force or forces. This is normal, but not everything in science can be explained this way. There are a few significant exceptions to this rule in science. God is one of those, but not the only one, and that's what's important.

For example, in nature, the Earth attracts the moon because of gravity, and electrons attract protons because of electromagnetism. Thus, any motion can be explained by a force, but how can we explain the force itself? A long time ago, it was believed that the planets moved because angels were flapping their wings behind them, but the truth is that the forces of nature cannot be explained, nor will they ever need an explanation. They simply are, and, in this sense, God's existence can be understood as a force of nature that cannot be explained in reference to any other force in the universe. The proof for such a force can be derived from the influence it has over nature, just as we do with any other fundamental force. This means that the evidence for God is what God has created and, as long as that cannot be explained by any other force or with the complex interactions of many forces, God would have to suffice as an explanation for the phenomena of life that we believe he created. One major difference between God and any other law of nature is that God's actions cannot be observed, just like the actions of a sculptor from ancient Greece could not be observed, but we can still infer the existence of both a sculptor and a God from the things they have created. If God is not acting in a way that would influence the world today, then naturally we cannot expect to observe his influence directly, but the same could not be said from a gradual process such as evolution. You cannot expect to meet Picasso or Rembrandt or ask questions from them, but you can still expect mountains to grow and continents to drift, even if by only a little bit. Even if God is still around, if he only adds new organisms to the gene pool of Earth once every few million years, then we really can't expect to see his handiwork in the near future.

As God is so elusive, it is easy to see how God as an explanation can be easily abused to explain anything and everything, but it is the knowledge of such detrimental features that can prevent use from going too far when attributing too many phenomena to God. In the past, when lightning hit a tree, it was believed that Zeus or Thor was directly responsible for that phenomenon; however, through the accumulation of knowledge, science has determined that divine intervention was not the cause and different forces were actually responsible. So, this God hypothesis could be and has been defeated, despite the difficulty involved in trying to observe a supernatural being in action. It can be easily understood why people can dislike an explanation that involves God, owing to the many instances of incorrect attributions throughout history. Many see any reference to a God as a God of the gaps argument, or as an argument from ignorance, but the problem with such counterarguments is that they can be made, regardless of whether God exists or not, and even if we have a legitimate reason to believe that he does. If, for example, lightning would strike multiple times in a forest and burn several trees in a way that, if we flew over them in a helicopter, we could see "God was here!" as a message written in fire, one could still argue that claiming that God was literally there, is a God of the gaps argument and, therefore, should be dismissed accordingly. I would argue that if we attributed such an event to the undirected causes of nature, rather than the conscious actions of an intelligent being, we would not be doing science and ourselves a favor. There can be legitimate reasons why the existence of an entity, such as God, can be stipulated in science and the as-of-yet unexplained origin of life is one such reason.

You can also think of God as a catastrophe, like the eruption of a volcano, which can happen, has happened, and will happen, but it is probably not happening right now. An act of God only happens from time to time, but when it happens, it dramatically alters the landscape where it happens. Even if you cannot see an eruption right now, you can always see the remnants of a volcano's eruption. The ash it brings and the stone it creates remains detectable long after an eruption, even though by that time, the volcano might no longer be active. In principle, God works in a similar fashion. He makes living beings, and the descendants of those organisms or their remains can still be detected today, but that doesn't mean we can expect to be able to observe creation itself. If God is a force of nature, it is a force that is very similar to that of a volcano, sparse and unyielding. I believe this analogy is very fitting because it was Charles Lyell who defeated the catastrophist view of volcanoes using his principle of gradualism, and it was this methodology that Darwin later copied to defeat creationism. It is only fair that God is now being used to challenge Darwin's idea. Unfortunately, catastrophism is a very vague science, just like the theory of evolution, which is one of the reasons why both could survive for as long they had. Some catastrophes can be observed, such as volcanoes, earthquakes, and tornadoes, but some are so rare that we can only speculate about their exact nature. Our Earth has undergone multiple phases since its existence, and some of the mutations of the Earth's surface would be really difficult to explain via a direct reference to causes now in motion, which includes common catastrophes of nature as well. God seems to fit into this category of forces that cause rare mutations, even though the act of creation, unlike everything else, is not bound by the laws of nature.

Generally, identifying new fundamental forces of nature and formulating them into laws has been only done in the field of physics. Only in the microscopic realm of quantum mechanics and in the great expanses of astrophysics have forces been found, and no other fundamental force has been located by any other scientific discipline. Physics, after all, is the science that deals with the fundamentals of nature, so it should come as no surprise that it is responsible for discovering all the fundamental forces of our universe. Thus, if we propose that God is also a fundamental force of nature or something similar, then it would be quite surprising if we didn't reach that conclusion through discovery in physics, and yet that is the exact opposite of what we have proposed. It is in the field of biology that we have argued for God's existence, which would be unprecedented, not just for biology, but for all other fields of study, except for physics. One definitely should not expect to find a fundamental force in biology, but as we will see, this is not as surprising one would think. Physics as a science deals with both microscopic and macroscopic phenomena, but it doesn't really concern itself with anything in between. It is simply assumed, and usually for a good reason, that everything we can observe directly on Earth can be explained by, or reduced to an explanation of, a combination of quantum mechanics and general relativity. This makes sense; however, physics doesn't really take into consideration the complexity of physical objects and whether they fall within the expected values predicted by the algorithm of the universe because in physics that could never be an issue. This being the case, physics has a blind spot when it comes to biological complexity because it simply doesn't have the tools to handle entities on that scale. Hence, it should make sense that God is not found inside physics but in a completely different field of science. After all, the reason why God's existence can even be justified is only because of the contradiction between the laws of nature and organic life forms that shouldn't exist in nature, and in physics, there's no possible way to find a contradiction like that.

Some arguments, such as the fine-tuning argument of the universe, which argues that nature is so fine-tuned to facilitate the existence and propagation of life that it must have been created by a god, contradict the argument from complexity. The fine-tuning argument is often used alongside other arguments in support of the existence of a god; however, in our case, invoking fine-tuning would be a mistake. In fine-tuning, rather than arguing that life is too complex to be created by the simple laws of nature, it is argued that the universe itself is too specific (in other words, too complex) to be created as is, by whatever created it. Invoking god to solve this predicament merely moves the problem from one place to another and, because god has to be as complex or greater than the universe, a good solution cannot be gained through this argument. It is always easier to argue for a fine-tuned universe than for a fine-tuned god, and the former will always be the simpler proposition among the two and, ultimately, the preferred one. It may be true that the universe was fine-tuned so that it would facilitate the survival of life, but this statement could not be used to prove God's existence. Then again, if God's existence has already been accepted, thanks to some other theories, then such consideration could help to determine the extent of God's power over the universe. Arguing from a god and arguing for one is not the same. We could ask why the universe is the way it is if a god created it, but that's different from arguing that a god must exist because the universe is the way it is.

Over the past few centuries, many arguments were used to deny the viability of God's existence, but most of these attacked the theistic God of religion rather than the deistic God that I am proposing in this book. Therefore, I will only deal with a few refutations of God's existence, as the rest don't seem to apply to the concept of a generic god. One popular argument claims that if a more complex being is necessary to create complex organisms, then that more complex being would also require a creator that is even more complex, and so on to infinity. An endless loop of creation would not make much sense, of course, so this argument may seem valid at first, but if we look carefully at the argument's premise, we will see that it suffers from some significant flaws. Remember, we argued for God's existence based on the assertion that the universe is too simple to create complex organisms, but that was based on the laws of nature and not on the laws of super-

nature. The forces that exist in supernature may be sufficiently complex to have been able to create a god or even
many gods; this could have been even accomplished by a
process that is evolutionary in nature, as the same limitations
that apply to our universe do not apply to God's universe. It is
also possible that God has always existed and has always
possessed the complexity that is required for the creation of
life. Either way, it doesn't make much difference. What
matters is that the greater universe, which includes all of existence, both nature and supernature, had and has a definite
amount of complexity and, just as the complexity of our
universe does not require an explanation, neither would the
greater universe need one. Some complexity is always needed
for existence, and it makes no sense to put an arbitrary limit
on how much there can be. Whether that is an amount
claimed to be based on the known laws of nature or equal to
nothing, as some believe, ultimately, it is simply not right to
create such limits for nature in science. Nature exists, and it is
what it is and exists because it exists. That is all the explanation we should need for why it exists and how much stuff may
be inside it, and how complex all of that must be.

Another interesting objection to God is the one based on
the size of the known universe relative to Earth and the solar
system, which argues that an omnipotent creator would not
need to create so many stars and planets to create life. This
objection rests primarily on God's attribute of omnipotence,
which is fundamentally a theological concept because, even if
such a thing was possible, it would still be an attribute that,
like nothingness, could not be observed in any shape or form.
Even if a god was all powerful, we would never be able to tell;
therefore, it doesn't even make sense to make such claims to
begin with. If we remove the necessity of omnipotence from
the argument, then this objection can still be raised, which is

why I have chosen to share it here. The problem is that the claim, God would not make such a large universe to create life, can only be made in reference to human action, as no other intelligent being can be compared with God. Therefore, the real question is whether a human would make such a large universe to create an insignificant pebble such as Earth or not? I believe that the answer is unequivocal "yes," as we had made things that have been much larger than they might have needed to be. Look at the Super-Kamiokande (SK) neutrino detector, for example. The SK was built a thousand miles below the Earth's surface and consisted mainly of a tank roughly 40 meters high and 40 meters wide. This tank holds 50,000 tons of ultrapure water and sits atop 13,000 light detectors to catch the universe's most insignificant elementary particle, a neutrino. This particle is so light and so unresponsive that it is almost impossible to detect in the sea of radiation that is constantly bombarding the surface; however, deep underground, with a large number of detectors, there's a chance that we might catch one from time to time. If tomorrow an alien came to earth and saw the SK detector, it might well ask: "Why did you build such a huge system to catch such a small insignificant thing?" The answer would be based on probability, that is, how big it needs to be to catch a neutrino. The reason why God created a universe as large as ours might be similar to why our neutrino catchers are so large. After all, what is the probability that the right type of sun and the right type of planet will be created at the right distance from each other to be ideal to host life for a very long time. In other words, how many star systems and galaxies were needed to be created in the Big Bang to reliably get at least one of each that fits the criteria required to sustain life? Quite a lot, I think. If God did not have unlimited resources, which he most likely didn't, and was bound by the laws of his own universe, which he most likely was, then can we really suggest that there can be no reasonable explanation for why he created such a large universe?

Perhaps, if God has created our universe, then the purpose of his creation must have been to create life and for that everything had to be set just right so that life could survive for an extended period of time. I call this assertion the life-centered view of the universe, and while it isn't really necessary to make the argument for God, I do think it makes the most sense if God's existence is already a given or at least implied. This is a view and not an argument, as an argument like fine-tuning could never be considered scientific, regardless of how convincing it may sound. It may be true that the rules of the universe were created by God so that life was easy to create and sustain, but the fact that life is being sustained doesn't prove that the universe was created by a god. That said, it is very interesting to think what choices God might have had when creating the universe, if his ultimate goal was to create life and nothing else.

Chapter 11

A Story of Creation

Inventing stories of how life might have risen has been a long-standing tradition of both science and religion, and I am inclined to continue this tradition so that I can demonstrate how easy it is to create such stories. Just as naturalists have crafted a story that fits their worldview, so can anyone create one that fits theirs. The only criteria, it seems, is that the story must be consistent with the facts revealed by science, to the extent that the story does not contradict the naturalist's worldview itself. You would only need to read or listen to how biologists explain the evolution of the eye to confirm this proposition. Anything that contradicts the worldview is disregarded, and, as such, I am confident that we can create a story that meets the criteria used in evolutionary biology.

As we have established that our theory of natural creation argues for God as the *de facto* creator of life and probable creator of the known universe, based on the life-centered world view of the universe, we will start from the beginning from the creation of the universe itself. Our assumptions are as follows: there is a God, an intelligent being with some powers, who used those powers to create a universe so that he could make life. Why he wanted to create life is a question we cannot answer, but if we could, it would have to come from an understating of what life is and what utility it may have for God. There is no clear benefit for God to create life, but the same could also be said for people creating art or games. Such things do not increase the survivability of humans directly and yet it would be unfair to claim that they do not possess utility. Perhaps, the same is true for God and his relationship to living beings, as life may be nothing more than a work of art created by God or a game for him to enjoy. Voltaire once wrote: "If God did not exist, it would be necessary to invent him" and he may be right, but what if God thought the same about life: "If life did not exist, it would be necessary to invent it," and so he did invent it.

If you had to describe what life is on a fundamental level, as simply as possible, what would you say? It is an entity that consumes matter or a thing that can be changed, and energy or the thing that can change things, and replicates itself through the process of using energy to transform matter. So, we need two things, the thing that can change and the thing that can change things; in other words, matter and energy. We need a lot of both of these things but, as energy is something that can change things, it is naturally a threat to matter, which can be changed, and so is a threat to life itself as well. This means that energy and matter have to be separated, but not completely, because if we did that, life would be impossible. We need a relatively constant supply of energy that transfers consistent amounts of nonthreatening energy to the matter that will be used to make life. In other words, we need a sun and an Earth. If a proper, life-sustaining combination of the two is difficult or improbable to make, then we need many, many suns and Earths. And those many suns should not collide, so they need to move predictably and have a lot of space in between them, just like in our galaxy. And, we also need something that will create the many kinds of stuff that will be required to make life, like a supernova that blasts all types of chemicals into empty space from which planets can be formed that will (or at least some will) follow the movement of the stars. Moreover, if all of this could be created by establishing a few simple rules, then that would be really nice, even if a lot of unnecessary things would be created as a by-product of the simple rules or laws. We can see that most of the larger things in our universe like stars or planets are things that we absolutely need for life, and there isn't really that much in existence that we don't need. This is why it is interesting to think about how God could have created a different kind of universe and whether such a creation would have enhanced the ability of life to survive or if this was the best God could do.

Once all the energy sources in the form of stars and all the sources of matter in the form of planets are in place, God only needs to find a suitable solar system with a suitable sun and planet pair before he can seed life on the planet. For the sun, it is important that it is able to send a relatively constant amount of energy to the planet for an extended period. For the planet, it is imperative to be at a distance that is neither too close to nor too far from the sun. If the planet is too close, then all the water will evaporate, while if it is too far, it will freeze. Neither possibility is favorable for organic life. There are a few other factors God would have to consider when selecting the ideal solar system; however, what ultimately matters is that our solar system was undoubtedly a prime candidate for hosting life and, therefore, it is not strange that God chose it to be the host. One remarkable feature of Earth, other than its magnetic field and gigantic moon, is the abundance of water found on its surface, the origin of which has been a hotly debated mystery for some time. Regardless of its true origin, God would probably not find it difficult to transport large volumes of water to Earth sometime after the planet formed. Therefore, we can assume that it is within God's power to send large objects, such as giant asteroids made of ice, crashing them into the Earth to deliver water. How such an event might happen may be difficult to imagine, but it would most likely be a miracle in which a specific kind of matter would appear, with all of its dynamic properties such as location, speed, and movement direction, set in advance. To us, it would appear as if something came out of nothing, so if we ever saw this happen, we would probably be able to identify such a miracle as long as we were aware of the possibility of its existence. In all honesty, the idea that God had to create ice to bring water to Earth is a somewhat self-defeating argument, given how much he could make without direct intervention; thus, a purely naturalistic source is more preferable, but the possibility of a miracle happening should be still considered.

A miracle by its very nature must always be something that is out of the ordinary and unexpected. If it could be predicted with the same confidence, we can forecast the movement of planets, it would no longer be a miracle. While miracles are not something we can experience, or expect to experience, there are objects on Earth that resemble the act of miracles in some sense, even on Earth. If we imagine the universe as a computer simulation and assume that this simulation was created to entertain its creator in the form of a game, then we will find that similar simulations already exist in our world. For example, we can look at a computer game, such as a massively multiplayer game or MMO, for what a virtual reality may look like. It is important to look at a virtual world that was created with a purpose other than to be simply observed, as the latter leaves too much room for bias. A massive multiplayer online game is more ideal in this regard, as its purpose is to entertain and not to inform.

MMO games connect thousands of players and allow them to put their virtual characters or avatars into the same virtual world. These worlds often resemble our reality in some aspects, but they are always much simpler than ours and the freedom of the characters are also more limited, regardless of how it might seem to the actual players controlling them. In an MMO, things come into being or disappear into nothingness all the time. It is normal. If something is needed, it is created, and if it is no longer needed, it is destroyed, sometimes temporarily and sometimes permanently. If our universe was also a computer simulation, it would be really easy for its creator to bring into or remove from existence anything they may desire.

However, in this scenario, it would be quite difficult to defend the life-centered view of the universe because if everything was a simulation, then it would not make sense for God to make so much stuff if his only goal was to make life on Earth. Thus, this possibility is unacceptable, but it may still be okay to think of the universe as a simulation—just not one that is run on any type of computer that we are familiar with. Rather than thinking of this computer as a general-purpose problem-solving machine, it is, perhaps, better to see it as a machine designed for a specific task and, therefore, was built with a specific framework and parts in mind. It is more like a part of a computer, like a video card that has a specific task and architecture designed for that task, rather than the central processing unit (CPU), which is designed to solve any task at any time. While the CPU of a computer is capable of running the same calculations as a graphics card does, it is nevertheless much less efficient in doing those calculations than a graphics card. Conversely, a graphics card cannot function as a CPU, or even without one, despite having very similar circuits.

Although our universe is most likely not a computer simulation, it is still interesting to think about what it would mean if it were and, moreover, whether we could tell that it is if it was, in fact, a simulation. If it was a simulation, or something very similar to one, then it wouldn't be impossible for God to alter the simulation and introduce new things into the system at any point he may desire. Games like the aforementioned MMO's are created by programmers and artists, but once they are created, neither can influence the evolution of the game world or the experience of its players directly. If something breaks or a player is stuck for some reason, or if someone is cheating in the game, the programmers simply can't help because the creators of the world don't have the means to change the rules while the simulation is in motion. In a multiplayer game, however, there exists a group of people whose job is to handle such situations and have been granted explicit powers by the developers to accomplish such tasks. They are called game masters or GMs for short. They can do things that regular players cannot. They have the ability to move anywhere in the game; they can create items or any other game object from thin air and place them wherever they like. They can move unseen by players, except for other GMs, but they can see everything that the regular players do in the game. The game master's actions in a game are analogous to a miracle in the real world. It is rare, seemingly spontaneous, and defies the established laws of the world in question.

Most companies, as an official policy, limit the actions of their GMs to the bare minimum necessarily needed to help their customers. After all, they are not supposed to be there, at least not canonically. God's interactions with our reality might be intentionally limited for the same reason. After all, if God's goal is to seed, alter, and develop life on Earth, then demonstrating his power to a bunch of apes is probably not very high on his priority list. It would be perfectly reasonable for God to act through a miracle only once or twice every million or so years to adjust creation only when necessary. We must also consider the possibility that God is limiting his influence on purpose to preserve the delicate balance of nature. After all, we are talking about a being that might have brought the known universe into existence; so, any action that is by any estimation less drastic than that will be, by definition, limited. Maybe this is why nature is both self-governing and self-sustaining. Perhaps, that fact is a reflection of God's intent to not interfere more than necessary. The less interference there is, the more predictable the experiment will be, and the less likely it will go haywire. The only policy God seems to follow is a principle of minimalism, so that will be an important guide for our story of creation.

When nature and its laws have been established, the galaxies, stars, and planets have aligned, and a desirable planet was found, and the means to affect that planet established, God could finally begin creating life. Creating a being in our universe that can sustain itself almost indefinitely, even in a simple form, is not an easy task. The simple laws that govern nature force everything to drift from order to disorder, and life must constantly fight against it. Life needs to fight entropy and constantly renew itself in the process of death and rebirth. God, therefore, integrates an orderly death into every living being, rather than fight the disorderly demise of entropy.

As we can observe a general increase in the complexity of organisms over time, it can be safely assumed that one of the objectives of God is to create complex living beings that, unlike simpler beings, cannot survive on the pre-organic, barren planet Earth. Thus, one of the tasks God must achieve is to create simple organisms that will terraform the planet. It is plausible to suggest that these life forms did not come into being on Earth and were simply transported there from some unknown origin in space, as that way the integrity of our planet would be much less threatened when God brought this new matter into existence.

Once God can safely create and transport matter to Earth, he creates organisms like the *Cyanobacteria*, which use the energy from the sun through the process of photosynthesis to break water and create oxygen. Over 400 million years, the oceans become dense with oxygen in the Great Oxidation Event, which allowed different microorganisms that burn oxygen including multicellular bacteria to survive and flourish. In the next billion years, as the oceans and the lands on the surface reach peak oxygen density, the oxygen slowly spill out into the atmosphere, making life possible on both land and in the sea. Around 300 million years after oxygen started to accumulate in the atmosphere, the Cambrian explosion begins. During this time, large and complex organisms were created that will be the precursors to every animal, plant, and fungi on Earth.

As higher forms of life seem to be much more closely related than these former organisms, or at the very least just as closely related as the former, it is safe to assume that they were not transported to Earth in their current form. It is much more likely that only the genetic information was moved to our planet and that new species were created by injecting the new genes into some designated preexisting specimens. This could have been attained by purposefully designed viruses, but it is also possible that God used some other means we have yet to encounter to create the new species. Either way, the goal of creating higher forms of life was within arm's reach for God.

Complex living beings are very delicate compared with lower forms of life. The environment they live in needs to be controlled a lot more than for archaea or bacteria, which are ironically responsible for most of the environmental control that higher forms of life need to survive. Even though most privileged living beings, like animals, can survive in a spectrum of environments, that spectrum is, in fact, extremely narrow. Once the terraforming is complete, it is extremely important that the status quo does not change; otherwise, the consequences will be dire for numerous organisms that rely on it. These most-vulnerable organisms are, arguably, the most important to God. Any mistake that disturbs the delicate balance of the biosphere can easily lead to the mass extinction of higher forms of life. Such events have been a regular occurrence since and even during the Cambrian Period. It is not rare to see close to half of all species dying in a mass extinction event every 50 to 100 million years, although they have become less frequent as time progressed. This begs the question of whether these events were accidental or an intentional ploy by God to get rid of a large set of living species. Were these events, perhaps, orchestrated to make room for new candidates or to see which were strong enough to survive even a mass extinction? It is possible that God created numerous prototypes before he would decide what to keep, and it was necessary to level the playing field a few times during this process. It is also possible that the stability of Earth's climate in the past was simply not consistent enough to sustain the reproduction of most complex living beings, and so most died out naturally, perhaps against the will of God.

To sustain an ecosystem, God must have created a circle of life that is completely self-regulating and will never run out of steam as long as the sun shines. This means there is a need for a circulation system that will keep the concentration of gases in the atmosphere and the elements in the earth and water constant. The oxygen use of animals and other forms of life creates carbon dioxide; therefore, it is necessary to create an organism that will split the carbon dioxide back into carbon and oxygen, so that others may breathe and eat. On land and in the sea, this is mainly done by plants and phytoplanktons, which produce oxygen via photosynthesis from air molecules rather than from water, and carbohydrates from the carbon. Given that the main task of these organisms is to supply essential chemicals for the rest of the ecosystem, it is vital that they do so efficiently. The sun is a very reliable energy source, but to convert the most sunlight into biofuel, organisms need to cover as large a surface area as possible. A large chunk of the surface is land and, despite the difficulty of capturing solar energy outside of water, it would not make sense to not utilize the energy that hits the continents daily.

To utilize all the light that hits the Earth's surface, God must create organisms that can survive on land and, simultaneously, be engaged in the same photosynthesis process as phytoplankton. God must, therefore, create plants. For plankton, it is not difficult to find food, as they can simply drift with the waves, but for plants, this is a much more difficult problem. Organisms need more than just sunlight and air to photosynthesize. Plants need to build and sustain their own tissues and multiply, just like any other organism, and for this reason, they must consume specific chemicals from nature. In water, it is relatively cheap to find nutrients, as they tend to just float around and so do planktons; however, on land, it is not so simple and plants can't simply look for food as that would waste energy. Plants need to be immobile, which as far as sunlight is concerned is not a problem, but to be able to consume nutrition, a new network of organisms is required, and to make that possible, God has to create soil.

Soil is essentially a hub of organisms whose purpose is to break down any useful matter into nutrients that the plants may consume through their roots. Making soil is an extremely difficult process, but it is necessary for anything on land to survive, and that is why we have so many microorganisms involved in making soil or using it to feed the plants somehow. For example, mushrooms are uniquely adept at breaking down organic matter and use the surplus and their mycelial network to supplement the diet of plants. By creating soil, God has solved the inefficiency problem plaguing photosynthesis on land, but by making plants stationary, a new issue that is not related to nutrients has appeared. One problem with sexually reproducing organisms, which includes plants, is that the organisms normally need to be able to meet to exchange their DNA. With plants being stationary, and the soil not being really ideal for transferring DNA from one plant to the next, a new solution is required to facilitate sexual reproduction between them. As producing DNA and a container that can safely store it does not require lots of chemicals, God's first solution was to simply move DNA in the form of pollen, using the power of wind and even water to a lesser degree. While this solves the issue of plants not being able to sexually reproduce, it once again creates a new problem.

While pollination via wind is a viable strategy, the chances of a single grain of pollen reaching its destination are extremely low; thus, a lot of pollen needs to be produced for a single grain to find its target. Given how many plants there are in an area, the amount of pollen produced can reach levels equivalent to some forms of air pollution. Wind pollination is not just wasteful; it can also be harmful to the organisms that breathe it in from the air. God's solution for this problem was to, yet again, create a set of organisms that would mitigate the issue; in this case, these organisms would target plants and carry the pollen from one to another, usually by flying between them. The first of these organisms would be insects. While pollination may not have been the first task insects had to accomplish, it is certainly the most crucial, and they do a remarkably good job doing it. For example, the structure of a honeybee colony revolves around the need to pollinate as many plants as possible in the least amount of time. The social structure of the colony, the number of bees in a colony, and the physical structure of the hive have all been set with this goal in mind. Of course, this also means that plants must change as well, as all the insects and other animals need to be able to find where the pollen is and where it needs to go on the plant. And so, God created flowers, which are a kind of colorful bullseyes that guide insects to their center where the pollen is generally located. God has created many plants and many animals to pollinate them, and by doing so, the energy shortage on land was, for the most part, solved.

Given that God has now created a self-sustaining power plant on land and on sea, the next task is to use that power for something meaningful. The first step is to create animals that will consume the plants and plankton, burn what they consumed using oxygen, and use the energy produced to move and power their bodies. The ability to move is also useful for sexual reproduction, as nonstationary organisms are able to seek and court their mates. Movement is especially important on land, while in water it is less important. For example, corals, which are animals, are fine being stationary. For land animals, moving from plant to plant to eat is necessary because, unlike plankton, plants don't simply wander into the mouths of animals. Unfortunately, this means that most animals must eat frequently to offset the high energy cost of moving around. While this is generally fine, if God wanted to create an animal with a specific purpose in mind, the fact that animals have to spend so much time eating to sustain themselves could potentially hinder his plan. For some specific tasks, therefore, a new kind of animal was needed, one that didn't consume plants, but rather something else.

While plants are able to conserve energy, the true kings of storing food are the plant-eating animals themselves. Unlike flora, which needs to cover a large area of the surface to efficiently utilize the sun's energy, they can simply consume the energy that the plants conserved over time. By moving around and consuming all the plants in an area, or parts of the plants, they can store high amounts of potential energy in the form of carbohydrates or fat in their bodies. Essentially, they, too, can become the source of food for other organisms, the same way plants serve as food for them. We are referring to the organisms that eat other animals as predators or carnivores, and, unlike their prey, they do not need to spend nearly as much time eating as their plant-eating ancestors did. Alternatively, some animals can also eat the nutritionally dense produce of plants, such as fruit, to gain an energy boost that is similar to what they'd gain from consuming meat; however, the availability of plants that produce fruit is naturally limited. Either way, God has created animals that now have more time to engage in other activities, such as guard a territory or socialize with each other. Predators also have the task to thin out the herbivores so that they do not over reproduce and also don't fall behind genetically relative to their ancestors.

Given that both the land and sea have been conquered by animals, it is only natural that God would want to conquer the last easily accessible place on Earth, the air. All kinds of animals were given the ability to fly, including, but not limited to, birds, insects, and mammals. Many airborne animals are utilized to pollinate plants, and their ability to do that is unmatched in the animal kingdom. Even some bats take part in the process, so it is probable that the idea of flying has come to be in God's mind for this purpose, but once the difficulty of flying was solved, he utilized it for other things as well. Flying requires a ridiculous amount of energy so it is no wonder that, other than insects, most flying animals are either predators or have a highly condensed food source, such as seeds or the nectar that they acquire in return for the task of pollinating plants.

God has created many species, and I have only referenced a small fraction of them. It has been estimated that about a trillion different mostly microscopic species exist on Earth. And why wouldn't he make so many? He had the time and the means to create an almost unlimited number of organisms. A being that has existed for billions of years has plenty of time to test out any creation of his and, if one does not work, there's always the next time. What would you have done if you had near-limitless power and time and a playground that only your imagination could bind? Is it, therefore, so strange that life is so diverse that we may never ultimately be able to catalog every species in the end? In nature, diversity is a strength because, even if one species dies out, there will be another to take its place. There is no microorganism, plant, or animal that cannot be replaced. Well, except for one.

God has created all kinds of organisms, large and small, aquatic and terrestrial, stationary and self-propelled, smart and not-so-smart, but all creatures he created were designed to survive and be bound by the environment he created. In other words, he created users and not makers, beings that are not allowed to exist outside their designated time and place. However, this changed relatively recently because God created something he never had in the past 4 billion years of guiding life's progress on Earth. God created humans. Now we may not be the only species to ever exist with the capacity to think rationally, form concepts, and modify nature to our needs, but we are certainly the most recent one, or at least the only one for the moment. Thousands of years ago, there had been several races of humans, but today only one remains. Us *Homo sapiens* (*H. sapiens*) are often credited with the forced extinction of other human species, but it may also be true that we had nothing to do with their demise. It is after all curious that, given how widespread modern humans became and how they took hold of most continents and many islands, not one different species of humans survived to the age of writing. Even today, in our technologically advanced and globally interconnected world, there are still tribes of humans living in complete isolation in places like the Amazon, and still no population of humans other than *H. sapiens* has ever been found. How can this be when humans have always been at any time above every apex predator, except for themselves? Shouldn't apes that are more closely related to humans be more likely to survive, rather than less likely?

Humans are more unique in nature than people give them credit for. They are *the* rational animal, not simply one of the rational animals. While many animals are born with the knowledge they need to survive, humans are born with a very limited set of instincts and aptitudes. Take language, for example. Every animal from the same species speaks the same language, regardless of where they were born. A honeybee from America, for example, has no problem communicating with a European honeybee. The same cannot be said about humans. Humans need to learn and, in rare cases, create their own language, and the aptitude to do so is one of the few things they are born with. You might ask, why is that?

Consider the fact that a rational animal has to be able to form new concepts as it needs to (and does) create new things. Therefore, God could not give humans a language with a specific set of words because that would limit our ability to reason. Alternatively, if God did not give us the ability to learn a language, then we would not be able to communicate with each other, and it would make concept formation even harder than it already is. God gave us an abstract language, but no words to use it with, so we had to fill in the blanks, which led to the creation of numerous languages and language families, as those languages diverged from each other. This, of course, made it more challenging for humans to communicate, but what choice did God really have? Lucky for us, humans have the ability to mitigate the issue of divergent languages so it is not all bad.

Humans are born with very limited knowledge. They are as close to a blank slate as a mammal with our attributes can be. This is intentional, as a rational being is meant to discover nature and, through discovery, understand it. A honeybee, on the other hand, is born with not just the aptitude to fly, but a complete language and the knowledge about how and when to build their hive. They know where to build their hexagon-shaped cells, how to stack them together, what material to use, and how to gather that material. They are also able to coordinate with each other so that they can build several hive cells at the same time. Bees are born with this knowledge, while humans are born with nothing of the sort, despite the apparent difference in the size of their brains. Humans have to learn everything, except how to drink milk and when and how to cry. Everything else has to be learned either instinctively or deliberately, as it should be for a rational animal. Even in artificial intelligence (AI) projects, there is a difference between AI that learns based on human action and AI that learns from its own actions because the latter, if it's possible to create, is always better than the former. Even if we only give the AI a base set of human actions or decisions and then let it make its own, the AI that can only learn from itself will outperform the one that learned from humans. Our AI is created to resemble a tabula rasa as closely as possible. That is how we humans create intelligence, and that is also how God created humans.

Given the prevalence of *H. sapiens* in the present and the many human-like species that came before it, is it possible that our cousins became extinct by design and not by our hands? If the species that are now extinct have not met the standard that God set for them, it is reasonable to believe that God simply got rid of them. Of course, that would have only made sense once the desired product was created, but after that, there was no need to keep the humans deemed inferior by God. It is possible that the human species of the past were merely prototypes for what came after and were ultimately only used as a template to create the ideal beings. It is also possible that we are not the final product and are simply the next step in God's plan to create the optimal rational animal. In that case, our human race might share the same fate as other human species and go extinct the next time God decides to do an upgrade. The fact that we are the only human species existing at this time should give us hope, as it would make more sense to have multiple species coexisting at the same time, to make experimentation easier. In the past, multiple human-like species existed along with humans, and the fact that we are the only ones who remain could mean that we are the final product.

Why did God create a rational animal? Was making an intelligent being the purpose of life, or was creating humans meant to serve the unknown purpose of why life was created?

Are humans a means to an end, or an end in themselves? We may never know, but we can always guess as that is what this chapter is for. Consider this: What if all the great extinctions in history were not intentional, but the result of great natural disasters that God could not prevent. If God did not wish for these events, then it follows that he would try to prevent them in the future, but what type of organism could possibly achieve such a thing? For example, what type of living being is capable of preventing a large asteroid from falling to Earth? Perhaps, it would be arrogant to claim that we can do that right now, but we are probably not that far away from being able to destroy or redirect large asteroids and we are the only living beings on Earth who could achieve such a feat. After all, no other species can even come close to us when it comes to destroying things that we don't like. We are number one, so is it far-fetched to think that God's purpose in designing humans was to protect life on Earth? Discounting the question of whether we are good at it and whether God has, perhaps, made a mistake in creating us, can we deny the possibility that God's original intention was to protect Earth by creating us? Even if we are not aware of this task, the fact that we need the Earth to survive, it would make sense from God's point of view that humans would have a natural inclination to protect it. A rational being would certainly come to that conclusion, but whether we have reached that point is debatable. We may never live up to the expectations of God. After all, at the end of the day, we tend to act more like animals rather than rational beings, and we may perish because of that, by our own hands or by God's, if we are not careful. God has given us a garden, his garden, and he made us the gardeners and, when he checks up on our work, he will decide whether we did a good job or not.

Alternatively, it is also possible that humans have no

special God-given role to fulfill, that humans are just another kind of animal, which are already too numerous to count. In the past, God made animals that were big, strong, or fast, and then he created one that is smart and uses his brain to survive rather than his claws or feet. As only one human species survived to the present day, even though this explanation may be plausible, it is certainly not preferable. In contrast, the possibility that humans have no special role to take in God's plan doesn't mean that humans are not special in God's eyes, or that there was no guiding principle that God followed to make us what we are. If the goal of creating the universe, the laws, the planets, and everything else was not simply to create organic life, but to create intelligent life, then God has already achieved his goal, and we would not need to live up to his expectations. Therefore, if we destroy ourselves, it is not God who we fail but only us. Thankfully, we have not yet reached that stage and, hopefully, we never will. It has been stated many times by different individuals that God created humans in his image, as well as the reverse: that humans created God in their own image. These statements may seem exclusionary, but they are not, and it is perfectly plausible that both are correct. If so, wouldn't it be more accurate to say that God has created god in the image of man as the one and only rational animal in nature? That would mean that there is still something for us to do, that if we want to reach true godhood, we must stop acting like animals and start being rational, because that is what a true god really is like.

Then again, that is also what a true human is supposed to be like. Possessing reason is what most differentiates us from other organisms and, therefore, our guide to action must always be based on reason, whether there is a god or not. In our world of abundance, where access to food is readily available, the need to think and act rationally has diminished for the common man. A thousand years ago, every person had to understand nature and their place in it to some degree; otherwise, they wouldn't have made it to the end of winter. People had to work hard and think about what work they needed to do the next day, if they wanted to survive. Today, most people from wealthy countries only need to think about where to go for a vacation. Compared with what our ancestors had to deal with, everything else is served on a silver platter. In recent decades, we have seen the rise of the so-called intellectuals, whose job is to think for us and tell us what to think, rather than encouraging us to think for ourselves. You might have heard the proverb, "Teach a man to fish and you feed him for a lifetime," but "teach a man to think, and he will stop listening to you" will never become one, because no intellectual would profit from that. Hence, nurturing our rational faculty should become our passion because with or without a god, if we stop thinking, we will inevitably end up on one of George Orwell's animal farms, assuming we are not on one already.

DEAR READER, I thank you for reading this book. I can only hope that it made you think about the mystery of mysteries of where species originate from. Despite my relentless critique of Darwin and his theory, I still consider him a great scientist and his work a crucial asset to scientific thought. After all, look at how many questions his theory made us ask about life and where it came from, which we might have never asked without him and his efforts to challenge the status quo. I am often reminded of what Darwin said in his autobiography regarding Herschel's Discourse:

During my last year at Cambridge I read with care and profound interest Humboldt's Personal Narrative. This work and Sir J. Herschel's Introduction to the Study of Natural Philosophy stirred up in me a burning zeal to add even the most humble contribution to the noble structure of Natural Science. No one or a dozen other books influenced me nearly so much as these two.

This book here is my humble contribution to the noble structure of Natural Science. I hope that one day you will add your own, if you haven't already, and if my book will ignite the burning zeal to contribute to science in a single person, then writing it was not in vain.

Afterword

In the introduction of this book, I gave you a quote from Christopher Hitchens speaking in favor of free speech at a debate from 2006. Here, I will provide you with the rest of that quote:

> One of the proudest moments of my life, that's to say in the recent past, has been defending the British historian David Irving who is now in prison in Austria for nothing more than the potential of uttering an unwelcomed thought on Austrian soil. He didn't actually say anything in Austria. He wasn't even accused of saying anything, he was accused of perhaps planning to say something that violated an Austrian law that says only one version of the history of the Second World War may be taught in our brave little tyrannian republic.

David Irving allegedly, and according to many historians, definitely is a Holocaust denier. In 2005, David Irving was arrested in Austria and later sentenced to 3-year prison time for the act of Holocaust denial he "committed" 16 years prior. Banning speech for whatever noble cause has long been considered to be wrong and shameful as no imitation of dark age zealotry could possibly be derived from the rights of man. Thus, spoke Zarathustra and so has Robert G. Ingersoll at the beginning of *Some Mistakes of Moses*, where he wrote the following in all caps: HE WHO ENDEAVORS TO CONTROL THE MIND BY FORCE IS A TYRANT, AND HE WHO SUBMITS IS A SLAVE.

You might believe that the history of the genocide of the Jewish people is unrelated to the theory of evolution, but in modern times, even evolution or rather evolution deniers have been connected to the great crime of the Sho'ah. For example, in The Greatest Show on Earth, Richard Dawkins compares evolution deniers to other history deniers:

> Imagine that, as a teacher of European history, you are continually faced with belligerent demands to 'teach the controversy', and to give 'equal time' to the 'alternative theory' that the Holocaust never happened but was invented by a bunch of Zionist fabricators.

I really hope that intellectuals will stop comparing people even if indirectly to deniers, not because it hurts my feelings, but because if I quoted this sentence from an actual denier and not Dawkins, I would be facing a 1-year prison sentence in my country. Hence, I believe we should be more careful who we call or compare to Holocaust deniers. I could also mention the social stigma and the violence committed against deniers, but those at least in the present are clearly overshadowed by the state's desire to deny them their rights. One notable exception in this regard is, of course the United States of America where the First Amendment of the Constitution prohibits Congress to make any law "abridging the freedom of speech, or of the press". As such, the state in America can only act when the speech poses an immediate danger to someone or someone's property. This would include, for example, the call to action to do violence, but Holocaust denial does not qualify as anything posing an immediate danger to anyone or anything, and so it cannot be banned there. Most European states do not protect speech the same way as the United States does and only tolerate free speech to some degree because if they didn't do so the chances of the ruling party getting re-elected would quickly diminish. It is a principle, but not the law or at least not a constitutional right, and that is why so many countries ban the practice of Holocaust denial in Europe.

The case of David Irving, whom Hitchens publicly had defended, is quite interesting in this regard. When I researched the person and his relation to the Holocaust, I found a large web of conspiracies spun from ignorance and hate, which would take an eternity to untangle, so I will opt to only share with you an abridged version. There are a few reasons why I think this is important: one is that Hitchens can no longer defend Irving, and second because his whole ordeal reveals a dire problem with Holocaust legislation, not counting the issue of free speech. That problem being that laws banning the denial of the Holocaust do not specify what the Holocaust and, consequently, what Holocaust denial is. It is left to a judge to define and decide what denial is and isn't, which essentially means that the judge will judge based on facts when the person is obviously guilty and on feelings when he/she is not. The same thing happens with juries, which is to say that the people the members of the jury tend to like, are far more likely to not get a guilty sentence than someone they don't like irrespective of the evidence presented to them. Given how notoriously unpopular David Irving is, it is no wonder why he has been found guilty of denying the Holocaust, but is he really a denier or merely a victim of circumstance and his own bad attitude?

Since my childhood, I have firmly believed that if someone is to be punished by any authority, he or she should be punished for something that they did, rather than something they didn't do, even if that something wasn't morally or legally wrong. That is my sole criteria because justice can be often a rare occurrence, in my opinion, and should not be expected to be found on every corner. This being the case if deniers are to be put into prison for their heretical views, the bare minimum the law should guarantee is for the individual to be actually guilty. For this reason, a legal standard should be used rather than prosecuting people willy-nilly and giving the judge absolute control over the matter. The basis of this standard would be a proper definition of the Holocaust and of what constitutes denial in relation to that definition. Even though I am absolutely against silencing dissent, I am more than happy to share a reasonable legal definition, if that meant that fewer people would be wrongfully prosecuted.

I will start from the Oxford dictionaries definition because that, even though a bit vague for legal purposes, is at least technically correct: "the Holocaust [singular] the killing of millions of Jews by the German Nazi government in the period 1941–5." I will add a few details and explain after that why my addition was necessary. My definition of the Holocaust is as follows: The planned killing of millions of Jews orchestrated by the leadership of the Nazi government between 1941–1945, predominantly on the Eastern Front and in the extermination camps of occupied Poland. This definition can be broken up into a list of statements: planned killing (of); millions (of people); (specifically) Jews; (orchestrated by the) leadership of the Nazi government; (between) 1941–1945; (on the) Eastern Front; (and in the) extermination camps (of occupied Poland). If a person denies at least ONE of these seven statements, that person is a Holocaust denier, and if a person denies none, he is not a Holocaust denier. The reason why these statements and these statements alone should be included is that no other statement is sufficiently significant that if denied even alone with all other statements declared in the positive, can be considered a denial of the whole of the Holocaust.

This definition has two or three controversial, purposefully vague statements. One of them is related to the number of victims and the other to the exact location of the killings, as well as the identity of the perpetrators. The reason why I and the Oxford dictionary does not put an exact number for the victims in the definition is that there isn't one. There are several estimates, some more accurate than others, but nobody can say for sure exactly how many have fallen victim to the Nazis. Take the founding father of Holocaust studies Raul Hilberg's book *The Destruction of the European Jews*, as an example. At the end of his book, there is a very important statistical summary called Appendix B. I will use this two-page Appendix B to make all my points. You could imagine the case that someone published these two pages of data without the rest of the book, in other words, without context, and the question is raised whether that is Holocaust denial or not. That might happen because the total number of victims, according to Hilberg's Appendix, is only 5.1 million, which is almost a million less than the official 6 million figure. Does this mean that Hilberg's a denier? I don't think so, and not because his calculations are erroneous, which if was the case, a judge wouldn't care anyway, but because the exact victim count is not that important, given the number is sufficiently large. After all, would we call someone a denier if they believed that only 4 million Jews were killed in the Holocaust? Could we say that, that person is trying to diminish the scale of the crime because he only believes the 4 million figure? Perhaps, but consider this: In Hilberg's Appendix, the 5.1 million figure includes a subsection called "Ghettoization and general privation" with a number of 800 thousand victims. This would normally mean death by disease and/or starvation, which is horrible, but does not carry a clear intent to kill from the guilty party. Intent is by definition absolutely necessary to prove any act of genocide. So, it is essential and that is why the word "planned" is in the main definition. If we take the text of the Appendix at face value—which is something a judge might do—then the figure of 5.1 million should be further decreased to a more "accurate" 4.3 million, which is closer to the aforementioned 4 million than the earlier figure of 5 or 6 million. So, what is the correct number? Is it 4 million or 5 or 6? I choose the answer that the number of victims was in the "millions," and I believe that there is no risk that a further revision to the definition might be necessary at any date in the future.

The other problematic part of my definition is the lack of specificity with regard to the location of the extermination camps. The ambiguity here is caused by the fact that the secrecy of the plan made it quite difficult to ascertain the exact location of every place of interest for a long time, and even today, we may lack names of places that we should know about. At the end of the day, it is simply not that important where exactly the extermination took place, at least from a legal standpoint. Would you call someone a denier because they claim that 6 million were killed, but deny that one specific camp was used for extermination? How could that possibly change anything in the grand scheme of things? Even the current list of camps today has been assembled after several revisions, and many camps that were on the list prior have been removed and are no longer there. Would we put someone behind bars for something historians got medals for in the past? Does that sound fair to you? The location of the camps and the names of the victims of each camp is important to the victims' relatives and for anyone who cares enough to seek out that information, but not for the legal system of a country that has banned Holocaust denial. The general place is crucial, of course. You can't say that the Holocaust took place in Antarctica and not in Europe, but other than that, the place is not materially significant to require a more specific statement to be added to the definition.

The third issue is that the definition does not mention a single perpetrator by name from the Nazi government. Here again, all we can state is that the exact number and identity of the killers and their supervisors are not known. Not every Nazi was involved in the Holocaust. It was executed in secret, and most didn't even knew about it when it was going on; therefore, specifying every single Nazi who was involved is not necessary as long as the group is correctly identified. Saying that the Nazis did it, but not X, Y, or Z does not make anyone a denier, but that doesn't mean that their statement is correct either. If you would say that all of it was done by aliens, then that would be an issue, but saying that a specific person was not involved does not make one a denier.

In light of the new and improved definition of the Holocaust I provided for the benefit of judges, and senior politicians who wish to prosecute speech, we can now ask the question of whether the writer David Irving is a Holocaust denier or not. To answer this question, I have checked what his detractors say about him, and I can say with confidence that none of their criticism is well-founded. At the moment, all of it is comprised of who knew about what, and what specific method of killing was used where, or was a specific camp a death camp or not. None of these qualifies as undeniable proof, and I can prove beyond any reasonable doubt that Irving is not a denier. David Irving has often been vague regarding the Holocaust, but when he isn't, he often talks about the SS Einsatzgruppen who were responsible for the killings on the Eastern front and about the Höfle telegram that the British have intercepted during the war.

The Höfle telegram lists four death camps known as the Reinhardt camps and the corresponding death toll of the killing operation for each camp until around the date the telegram was sent. This means that the numbers in the telegram underestimate the total number of victims for the whole of Operation Reinhardt. Not counting every victim for the whole of the operation, the total in the telegram for the four camps comes at 1.274.166. In Hilberg's Appendix, he estimates that for the full operational time of the four camps, a total of 1 million 550 thousand Jews were killed. Instead, in 2009, David Irving estimated on the basis of the telegram that 2.2 million were killed in the Reinhardt camps. The alleged Holocaust denier claims that 700,000 more people died in these camps than the father of Holocaust studies have claimed. For all extermination camps, Hilberg estimates that 2.7 million Jews have perished during the Holocaust. This means that in the worst-case scenario, Irving denied the killing of half a million people, which is only around half of the minimum or a quarter of the maximum that Hilberg denied in his Appendix. Worst-case scenario meaning by an estimate which is not applicable in a court of law or for anyone thinking reasonably. On a side note, I believe that the fact that Hilberg's estimates per camp conform to the numbers of the telegram to be the strongest validation of his work as a historian.

If I am being completely honest, in 2009, Irving said that he was only 80% certain that the Höfle telegram was genuine, but by 2014, that number increased to 100%, so at least by then, the witch hunt should have ended. There are numerous videos, articles, and letters in multiple languages that absolves Irving from the accusation of denial from at least 2009 onwards, and no evidence, on the contrary, has been found by me or anyone else for that matter. It is not difficult to see that Irving right now is not a Holocaust denier, and his critics only call him that because of ignorance or out of spite or greed, but what about the past? Was David Irving ever a denier to begin with? Just because his critics failed to mention a single valid instance of denial in the last decade does not prove that Irving was always innocent. We know what his stance was in the last 10 years, but what did he believe in the decade before or even before that? I dug deeper, and using the same definition I used to absolve Irving, I found that David Irving was most definitely without question a Holocaust denier in the past.

I found an old video recording of one of Irving's lectures, and in it, he denies not one but at least two critical aspects from my definition of the Holocaust. Now, I could tell you what Irving said or where to find this recording, but I don't like to wear stripes, and black and white is not my style, so I won't. Suffice to say that this event happened before I was born and many years before the Höfle telegram was found in the British archives. You might believe that is a valid excuse to absolve David Irving from guilt, and he certainly thinks it is, but from my point of view, it makes absolutely no difference if it is or not. I would like to highlight though that the idea that someone who spent half his life in historical archives changing his opinion based on a historical document found specifically in an archive, is not as strange as some people would like you to believe.

The video of Irving's lecture was made around the time when he was doing his speeches in Austria for which he would be put into prison 17 years later, when he went back to that "tyrannian republic". In the trial, Irving claimed that two decades earlier he made a mistake and he no longer believes what he did back then. This might have been true considering all that he said after he was released from prison; however, true or not, this raises a question regarding prosecuting thought crimes. Because, if you have changed your mind after you made your comments about denial, you must still go to prison even though you are no longer a denier. So, you can go to prison for Holocaust denial even if you are not a Holocaust denier, which is not something that can happen with other types of crimes. If you are a murderer, nothing you say or believe will change that fact, you are still a murderer, but thought crime is different, and the criminal justice system is not prepared to handle crimes of this nature. The enlightened liberal architects of the western legal system never imagined that one day there would be a need to put people into prison for being too offensive and so the concept of due process is simply absent in such legislation for the simple reason that it is fundamentally inapplicable to something that can only exist in a person's mind. How could a judge or a jury not have reasonable doubt regarding what an individual's thoughts are or have been in the past, without being able to read the person's mind? Reasonable doubt is a legal standard that cannot, has not, and will never be applied to thought crimes such as denial or any other verbal hate crime.

The only sensible sounding critique of Irving I could find

was that Irving claimed that his opinion on the Holocaust did not change, which is probably true, he probably said such a thing to a reporter, but he also claimed that it did change, and he claimed that under oath. Deciding to base one's decision on a single vague comment as opposed to taking into account the dozens of comments on the contrary and only believing Irving when it conforms to one's biases is not what an honest and objective critical thinker should do. I am not surprised that Irving is being haunted and harassed by a multitude of ideologues. I have said before that you should not expect to find justice on every corner, and if your name happens to be David Irving, you should not expect it anywhere or at any point in time. I would like to say that there is a special place in Dante's Inferno for those who falsely accuse others, but because I do not believe that inferno is a real place, I will say instead that there is a special place in my heart for the falsely accused. In case someone is wondering though, in the Divine Comedy, accusers go to the worst place in the eight of the nine circles of hell, where they suffer from different diseases for being a plague on society.

David Irving is just one of the many who had to suffer, as ever since the age of information began, it has become trivially easy to defame others, and that aspect of our time will probably never change. However, just as easy it has become to accuse others, speaking out against false accusations has become equally easy; therefore, it is up to the people who know the truth to stand up and fight this plague. I believe I have done my part, but I am sure there will be many who will disagree with me and would rather see Irving on a spike than rehabilitated, and to them, I would like to offer the final words of Cristopher Hitchens on this matter:

I can't find a seconder, usually, when I propose this but I don't care. I don't need a seconder, my own opinion is enough for me and I claim the right to have it defended against any consensus, any majority, anywhere, anyplace, anytime, and anyone who disagrees with this can pick a number... get in line... and kiss my ass!

THE END

Sources

Christopher Hitchens at the University of Toronto's 2006 Hart House Debating Club

The Pleasure of Finding Things Out starring Richard D. Feynman. 1981 Horizon BBC

Lyell, C. (1830). *Principles of Geology Being an Attempt to Explain the Former Changes of the Earth's Surface, by Reference to Causes Now in Operation*. John Murray,

Herschel, J. F. (1830). *A Preliminary Discourse on The Study of Natural Philosophy*. Longman Press.

Darwin, C. (1859). *On the Origin of Species by Means of Natural Selection, or the Preservation of Favoured Races in the Struggle for Life*. John Murray.

Darwin, C. (1887). *The Autobiography of Charles Darwin*. John Murray.

Dawkins, R. (2009). *The Greatest Show on Earth: The Evidence for Evolution*. Bantam Press. ISBN 9780593061732

Krauss, L. M. (2012). *A Universe from Nothing: Why There Is Something Rather than Nothing*. Atria Books. ISBN-10: 1451624468

Lodish, H., Berk, A., Matsudaira, P., & Kaiser, C. (2003). *Molecular Cell Biology* (Fifth Edition). W. H. Freeman. ASIN: B008BWZC5C.

Huxley, J. (1942). *Evolution: The Modern Synthesis*. MIT Press Academic.

Fischer, R. A. (1930). *The Genetical Theory of Natural Selection*. Clarendon Press. ISBN-10: 0198504403

The Darwinian Revolution starring Frederick Gregory, 2008. The Great Courses

Wolfram, S. (2002). *A New Kind of Science*. Wolfram Media. ISBN-10: 1579550088

Popper, K. R. (1963). *Science as Falsification*. Conjectures and Refutations. ISBN 9780415285940

Hawking, S., & Mlodinow, L. (2010). *The Grand Design*. Bantam Press. ISBN 9780553384666

Feynman, R. P. (1965). *The Character of Physical Law*. Modern Library. ISBN 9780679601272.

Lindberg, D. C., & Numbers, R. L. (2003). *When Science and Christianity Meet*. University of Chicago Press. ISBN-10: 0226482146.

Behe, M. J. (2007). *The Edge of Evolution: The Search for the Limits of Darwinism*. Free Press.

Meyer, S. C. (2009). *Signature in the Cell: DNA and the Evidence for Intelligent Design*. HarperOne. ISBN 0061472786

Dembski, W. A. (1998). *The Design Inference: Eliminating Chance through Small Probabilities*. Cambridge University Press. 0521678676 (ISBN13: 9780521678674).

Marshall, P. (2015). *Evolution 2.0: Breaking the Deadlock Between Darwin and Design*. BenBella Books. 1940363802 (ISBN13: 9781940363806).

Flew, A., & Varghese, A. (2007). *There is a God: How the World's Most Notorious Atheist Changed His*

Mind.   HarperOne.   0061335290   (ISBN13: 9780061335297).

Yahya, H. (1997). *The Evolution Deceit: The Scientific Collapse of Darwinism and its Ideological Background.* Translated by: Ahmad, M. Ta-Ha Publishers. 1897940971 (ISBN13: 9781897940976).

Ayala, F. J. (2009). *Darwin and the scientific method.*

Cannon, W. F. (1961). *The Impact of Uniformitarianism Two Letters from John Herschel to Charles Lyell.*

Orgel, L. E., & Crick, F. H. C. (1993). *Anticipating an RNA World Some Past Speculations on the Origin of Life: Where Are They Today?*

Daubin, V., & Szöllősi, G. J. (2016). *Horizontal Gene Transfer and the History of Life.*

Parrish, N. F., & Tomonaga, K. (2016). *Endogenized viral sequences in mammals.*

Bollenbach, T., Vetsigian, K., & Kishony, R. (2007). *Evolution and multilevel optimization of the genetic code.*

Van Hofwegen, D. J., Hovde, C. J., & Minnich, S. A. (2016). *Rapid Evolution of Citrate Utilization by Escherichia coli by Direct Selection Requires citT and dctA.*

Hilberg, R. (1985). *The Destruction of the European Jews* (ISBN 13: 9780841909106)

GNU/Linux Distribution Timeline by Andreas Lundqvist 2010

Long-Term Evolution Experiment (LTEE) at http://myxo.css.msu.edu/ecoli/

Lenski, R. E., & Travisano, M. (1994). *Dynamics of adaptation and diversification: A 10,000-generation experiment with bacterial populations.*

Tenaillon, O., Barrick, J. E., Ribeck, N., Deatherage, D.

E., Blanchard, J. L., Dasgupta, A., ... & Lenski, R. E. (2016), *Tempo and mode of genome evolution in a 50,000-generation experiment.*

Wiser, M. J., Ribeck, N., Lenski, R. E. (2013) *Long-Term Dynamics of Adaptation in Asexual Populations.*

De Visser J. A. G. M., Lenski R. E. (2002) *Long-term experimental evolution in Escherichia coli. XI. Rejection of non-transitive interactions as cause of declining rate of adaptation.*

Blount, Z. D., Borland, C. Z., & Lenski, R. E. (2008) *Historical contingency and the evolution of a key innovation in an experimental population of Escherichia coli.*

Blount, Z. D., Barrick, J. E., Davidson, C. J., & Lenski, R. E. (2012). *Genomic analysis of a key innovation in an experimental Escherichia coli population.*

Special thanks to the Darwin Correspondence Project at https://www.darwinproject.ac.uk/

Made in the USA
Middletown, DE
27 August 2022

72508239R00163